Berlitz®
South Africa

Text by Martin Gostelow and Ken Bernstein
Updated by Philip Briggs
Editor: Alex Knights
Series Editor: Tony Halliday

D0610901

Berlitz® POCKET GUIDE
South Africa

Fourth Edition 2005

PHOTOGRAPHY
All photography courtesy of South African Tourism; except Alamy: Mel Stuart/Westend61 p. 28, Stock Photos SA p. 50, Egmont Strigl/ImageBroker p. 61, Peter Titmuss p. 98; Paul Burton p. 72; John Warburton-Lee p. 97

CONTACTING THE EDITORS
Every effort has been made to provide accurate information in this publication, but changes are inevitable. The publisher cannot be responsible for any resulting loss, inconvenience or injury. We would appreciate it if readers would call our attention to any errors or outdated information by contacting Berlitz Publishing, PO Box 7910, London SE1 1WE, England. Fax: (44) 20 7403 0290; e-mail: berlitz@apaguide.co.uk www.berlitzpublishing.com

➤ Immerse yourself in the Zulu way of life at Shakaland in KwaZulu-Natal (page 54)

For spectacular views of South Africa's largest mountain range, visit the uKhahlamba-Drakensberg Park (page 46) ▲

Ostrich racing takes place in the Little Karoo (page 63) ◄

TOP TEN ATTRACTIONS

Taste the Cape's grape at the wine estates in Paarl and Stellenbosch (page 77)

◀ The breathtaking views from Table Mountain (page 71) complete a visit to Cape Town

One of Africa's truly great wildlife sanctuaries, Kruger National Park is a top destination for big game viewing (page 39) ▶

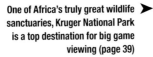

A classic arc of sandy beach, Plettenberg Bay (page 61) is one highlight of South Africa's vast golden coastline ▼

Marine life close up in the Two Oceans Aquarium (page 70) on Cape Town's waterfront

Look out from the southern tip of Africa at Cape Point (page 76) ▶

View South Africa's astonishing scenery from the luxurious carriages of the Blue Train (page 80) ▶

CONTENTS

A ➤ in the text denotes a highly recommended sight

Fact Sheets

INTRODUCTION

With remarkably diverse scenery, innumerable species of large mammals and birdlife, a rich floral kingdom and a cultural heritage rooted in three different continents, the Republic of South Africa, once known for its racial segregation, has evolved into one of the world's top tourist destinations.

A large number of international carriers fly direct to the country and, if you happen to be travelling from the UK, you'll avoid jetlag, as South Africa is just two hours ahead of GMT. A non-stop flight from London to Johannesburg – around 9,700km (6,000 miles) – takes about 11 hours. Direct flights to Durban or Cape Town take an hour or two longer.

While South Africa is the undisputed powerhouse of the African continent, with massive industrial and mining enterprises, a truly astonishing range of natural landscapes awaits the visitor: vast stretches of savannah brimming with herds of big game, wide bays and palm-lined beaches, a colourful diversity of wildflowers,

> An excellent way to explore South Africa would be to hire a car *(see page 105)*. Driving is on the left and English is spoken throughout the country. South Africans are keen travellers in their own land and expect high standards, so facilities are generally excellent.

towering rock amphitheatres, evergreen forests and semi-desert, vineyards and orchards. This variation is also reflected in the architecture, from Zulu beehive huts (which look like mud-and-thatch igloos) to gracefully whitewashed Cape Dutch mansions to the towering skyscrapers of central Johannesburg.

Sport is a serious passion in South Africa

Geography and Climate

South Africa's coastline stretches for 2,800km (1,740 miles) from the desert border with Namibia on the Atlantic coast, down around the tip of the continent and up to subtropical Mozambique beside the Indian Ocean. The coastline is mostly narrow, separated from the high inland plateau by a mountainous escarpment. Inland, South Africa borders Botswana, Zimbabwe and Swaziland, and surrounds the 30,355-sq km (11,720-sq mile) independent Kingdom of Lesotho.

Officially classified as semi-arid, in reality the climate varies as much as the landscape. While the large inland plateau, known as the Great Karoo, is extremely hot and dry in summer, the Cape Peninsula has a Mediterranean climate, with mild, wet winters and warm to hot summers. The seasons are exactly opposite to those in the northern hemisphere – great for sun lovers seeking winter relief. With plenty of hours of sunshine, any time of year can be the right time to travel,

Facts and Figures

Area: 1,212,100 sq km (468,000 sq miles).

Capitals: Pretoria (administrative), Bloemfontein (judicial) and Cape Town (legislative).

Population: 45,348,300; 24% speak isiZulu as mother tongue, 18% isiXhosa, 13% Afrikaans, 9% Sepedi, 8% English and 8% Setswana.

Provinces: KwaZulu-Natal (9,426,000), Gauteng (8,837,200), Eastern Cape (6,436,800), Limpopo (5,273,600), Western Cape (4,524,300), North West (3,669,300), Mpumalanga (3,123,000), Free State (2,766,800) and Northern Cape (822,700).

Government: The Republic has a constitutional democracy with a three-tier system of government. The national, provincial and local levels all have legislative and executive authority in their own spheres.

Religion: Christianity (almost 80%); Islam, Hinduism, indigenous beliefs.

Small herds of springbok are common in South Africa's arid northwest

but autumn (March–April) and spring (September–October) are particularly pleasant, when the weather's not too hot.

Exploring the Country

It was, perhaps, South Africa's world-class infrastructure that clinched the bid to host the 2010 football World Cup. The country has a very good network of roads, domestic air services link most sizeable towns, while the rail network ranges from quaint local services to the luxurious Blue Train *(see page 80)*. So, depending on time and taste, you can travel around South Africa by any combination of car, train and plane. Alternatively, you can hire a caravan, join a coach tour or even charter a helicopter. It's worth striking a balance between the cities and the countryside, and between culture and nature.

Johannesburg, a brash city built on gold, offers much in the way of shopping, eating and nightlife experiences, and the International Airport offers connecting flights to Cape

Town, Durban and the Kruger National Park. Another side of life can be experienced in the township of Soweto and, to the north west, you can visit the UNESCO-rated Sterkfontein Caves, sometimes known as the Cradle of Humanity for their hominid fossils. North of Johannesburg is attractive Pretoria, South Africa's capital city.

Over on the Indian Ocean, the city of Durban, Africa's largest port, is also a lively beach resort and surfing centre. In the Cape's southwestern corner, poised between the Atlantic and Table Mountain, cosmopolitan Cape Town offers a unique blend of European, African and Islamic culture. Around Cape Town are the principal centres of the South African wine industry, with great opportunities for wine-tasting and gastronomic pleasures. At the tip of the Cape Peninsula is one of Africa's best-known natural attractions, the dramatic seascape of the Cape of Good Hope.

The old clifftop lighthouse at Cape Point

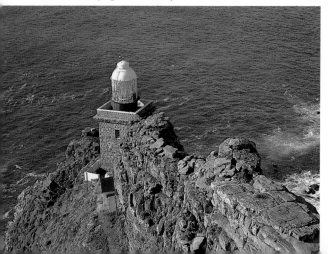

Ecotourism and Active Pursuits

Starved of tourism during the long years of apartheid, South Africa largely escaped the kind of environmental degradation that occurs in places with developed holiday industries. Today, conservation allows the state to guarantee the 'environmental rights' of citizens and reap the economic rewards of wildlife tourism. In fact, more wildlife roams the country today than a century ago, due to the

A guided game drive

state allowing private ownership of wildlife. And private game reserves adjoining the Kruger National Park have removed fences to allow freer movement of wild animals.

Little can beat the thrill of watching lions, rhinos, hippos and buffalo going about their daily lives in South Africa's excellent network of national parks and other game reserves. The country's varied landscapes offer all kinds of opportunities for viewing animals in their natural habitats. In KwaZulu-Natal alone you can watch hippos cooling off in the wetlands of Greater St Lucia, or white rhinos grazing in Hluhluwe-Imfolozi Game Reserve, or bottle-nosed dolphins playing in the surf off the coast.

South Africa's sports possibilities cover a lot of ground (golf, hiking, horse riding) as well as a lot of ocean (fishing, surfing, swimming). Rugby, cricket, football, boxing and horse racing draw the big crowds. Adventure tourism opportunities include hiking trails, white-water rafting, even bungee jumping and sand-boarding *(see page 87).*

Politics and People

Zulu father and son

From the late 1940s, when the policy of apartheid was codified, South Africa's National Party government pursued the goal of separate development of racial groups *(see page 20)*. This entailed the mass removal of citizens to new housing areas, a ban on intermarriage between the different race groups and the segregation of schools, hotels, buses, trains and even park benches. Many petty apartheid laws were repealed in the late 1980s, while the unbanning of the ANC in 1990 and simultaneous release of its most famous leader Nelson Mandela amounted to a tacit admission that the system the National government had enforced for almost half a century was both unworkable and immoral.

The majority of South Africa's 45 million inhabitants – almost 80 percent – are black, belonging to a number of nations or tribes, the biggest of which are the Zulu, Xhosa, Sotho and Tswana. Roughly one in 10 of the population is white, and slightly less than 10 percent are referred to as Coloured, meaning of mixed race. Another 2.5 percent are Asian, mostly the descendants of immigrants from India. White South Africans object strongly to being considered mere settlers or immigrants in Africa, especially those whose roots go back more than three centuries to the foundation of the Dutch station at the Cape. With them the Dutch language was introduced and from it evolved Afrikaans, the mother tongue of most South African whites and Coloured people. Nearly 40 percent of whites are native English-speakers, and English is understood almost everywhere.

A BRIEF HISTORY

Much of sub-Saharan Africa came late to the pages of recorded history, but it seems that our own species, Homo sapiens, first evolved on its sunny upland plains. Long before that, about 1,800,000 years ago, a type of ape-man known as *Australopithecus africanus* lived scarcely 30km (20 miles) northwest of the site where Johannesburg is now situated. Other fossil bones show that by 50,000 years ago a family that was recognisably human inhabited caves in Mpumalanga Province. Able to use fire and stone tools, these people were probably the ancestors of the hunter-gatherers responsible for the vivid rock paintings found all over southern Africa.

By the 5th century AD, migrating tribes from West Africa had brought an Iron-Age culture to much of what is now South

Prehistoric rock art depicts the early inhabitants of South Africa

Africa. When Europeans first came to Africa's southern tip they met other early inhabitants of the area – smaller, lighter-skinned people who hunted or herded cattle. They called the cattle-herders Hottentots and the hunters, Bushmen. Today they are classified as Khoikhoi and San; together, Khoisan.

When the first European settlers arrived in the mid-17th century, several black nations had migrated from the centre of the continent to southern Africa. There was little contact between them and the white settlers at the Cape until the mid-18th century. The Khoikhoi began to act as middle-men, but their numbers declined through war and disease until they finally faded away, blending into what has since become known as the Cape Coloured population.

The Dutch at the Cape

Following the first sighting of the Cape of Good Hope by Portuguese explorer Bartolomeu Dias at the end of the 15th century *(see page 76),* the Cape became a regular port of call for European, especially Dutch, ships. Here they could take on fresh water and barter iron, beads and brandy in exchange for local cattle. Sixty Dutch crew were forced to spend almost a year at the Cape when their ship was driven ashore in 1647. Once home, their leaders recommended setting up a permanent settlement to provide facilities for ships of the Dutch East Indies Company on the way to and from Southeast Asia.

On 7 April 1652, a party of about 100 men, led by Jan van Riebeeck, landed at Table Bay and began to build a fort and prepare land for

> As the settlement's need for labour grew, slaves were imported in the main from the Dutch East Indies (modern Indonesia). These slaves intermarried with Khoisan, Africans and the white settlers to form a new community, known today as the Coloured people.

A full-scale replica of Bartolomeu Dias' caravel in Mossel Bay

growing food. Despite clashes with the Khoikhoi, whose grazing lands were infringed upon, the settlement was established.

The colony kept its Dutch character even after the arrival of other nationalities, notably the French Huguenots, who added expertise to the Cape wine industry. The immigrants were obliged to learn Dutch, but they brought fervour to the Calvinist tone of the colony's Dutch Reformed Church. Thus was forged a new people: the Afrikaners, or Boers (meaning farmer in Dutch). Pushing further inland, many paid little heed to the authorities in Cape Castle, still less to those in Amsterdam.

Enter the British

Wars in Europe sent shock waves as far as South Africa. After a French attack on the Netherlands, the British occupied the Cape colony in 1795. They returned in 1806 and again, definitively, in 1814 as a result of territory exchanges following the Napoleonic wars. The change of government shook the foundations of Cape society. Britain outlawed the slave trade in 1807, abolishing slavery throughout the Empire in 1834. Faced with a curtailed labour supply, little compensation and the imposition of the English language and legal system, many colonials began to strike out into the wilderness. The pioneers were known as the Voortrekkers (literally, 'those who pull ahead').

Much of the land they took had been abandoned shortly before as a result of Zulu raids on other tribes. The Boers forced their wagon trains deep into the heart of the subcontinent. A new British colony on the Indian Ocean coast of Natal restricted the Voortrekkers to the interior, where they established two new states: the Orange Free State between the rivers Orange and Vaal and the Transvaal Republic to the north of the Vaal.

Citing bad government and ill treatment of the black population, the British took the Transvaal in 1877. However, in 1881, following news of a British defeat at the hands of the Zulus in Natal, the Transvaalers rose against their occupiers and forced them to withdraw. The clash of British and Boer interests grated quietly until the turn of the century, when it exploded in a second, much longer and more bitter war.

Fighting between white settlers and black tribes had continued on and off since the second half of the 18th century. Frontier wars with the Xhosa, for example, were fought every 10 years or so. The struggle for usable land

> Loss of life, land and power during the frontier wars devastated traditional Xhosa society, as they sought an explanation for these disasters. Nongqawuse, a young Xhosa prophetess, foretold that if the people killed all their cattle and destroyed all their crops, the dead would rise, new cattle would rise, and nobody would ever suffer again. Some 400,000 cattle were culled during 1856–7 and 40,000 Xhosa died as a result. They were no longer a force to be reckoned with.

The diamond rush in Kimberley left behind a vast gash in the earth

also underlay wars between black tribes, the most dramatic being those waged by Zulu general Shaka, the 'black Napoleon', who died in 1828. Zulu leaders fought the Voortrekkers, then the British, and it was only in the 1880s that British firepower imposed a kind of peace.

Glittering Hopes

In Hopetown, on the Orange River, the first diamond was discovered in 1866. The area was invaded by fortune hunters after a giant stone of 83.5 carats appeared, and the action soon shifted north to Kimberley, where finding diamonds was almost easy. Over the next 40 years, diggers went ever deeper, until Kimberley's Big Hole had yielded 3 tons of diamonds.

Gold had been found in various parts of South Africa, but the big strike came in the Transvaal in 1886 on the highveld referred to as the Witwatersrand, or Rand, which subsequently became the site of Johannesburg. The prospector sold his

The first president of the Transvaal depicted on a Krugerrand

claim for £10 and was never heard of again. The reef has since come up with more than 35,000 metric tons (32,000 tons) of pure gold.

Since 1881 Britain had kept her distance from events in the independent Transvaal, claiming only a vague right of veto over external alliances. However, with the Rand's riches unearthed, foreign prospectors and entrepreneurs soon flocked in.

The republic's government benefited from taxes levied on the *uitlanders* (foreigners), but denied them a voice in running the country. Cecil Rhodes, the mining magnate and prime minister of Cape Colony, plotted an uprising of the Transvaal *uitlanders*, but his accomplice, Dr Jameson, jumped the gun, leading an invading party from Rhodesia, which was quickly overcome by the better armed Boers. Three years later, in 1899, the British and the Afrikaners openly fought the issue.

The Anglo–Boer War

The Afrikaners were led at this time by the long-established president of the Transvaal – the bearded, top-hatted Paul Kruger. Three of his prominent military chiefs, Louis Botha, Jan Smuts and J.B.M. Hertzog, were destined to become prime ministers of the Union of South Africa. Although initially outnumbered by a ratio of five to one, the Boers held their own through innovative commando tactics.

British strategist Lord Kitchener employed harsh methods. Families of Boer soldiers were held in concentration camps. Some 26,000 inmates died, mostly of disease. Less publicised were the conditions in separate camps built for blacks, where the death toll was over 13,000. The revelations shocked British opinion and strengthened the inward-looking Afrikaners.

After two and a half years of fighting, the Boers conceded defeat in May 1902. Shortly after, Britain agreed to the formation of a self-governing dominion. They nevertheless managed to alienate the Afrikaners and did not attempt to extend the limited rights of non-whites that existed in the Cape and Natal.

The Union of South Africa, created in 1910, was an amalgam of the Transvaal and Orange Free State with the Cape and Natal, Britain's two colonies. So delicate were regional sensibilities that power bases were spread around the country, with Pretoria the administrative capital, Bloemfontein the judicial capital and Cape Town the seat of Parliament. Foreshadowing future policies it was decided that only whites could be elected as members of parliament.

Gateway to the South African Houses of Parliament in Cape Town

The World Wars and Aftermath

Only four years after creating the Union of South Africa the British Empire went to war with Germany. South African troops were quick to seize the German colony of South West Africa (present-day Namibia) and took a major part in the long campaign against German-led forces in East Africa.

By the time World War II broke out, Jan Smuts was in his second term as prime minister. Beating a powerful parlia-

Apartheid

Arguably, the path of racial segregation in South Africa can be traced back to the use of slave labour by white settlers in the 1650s. It was, however, in the 1950s that the systematic separation of the races was taken to its bureaucratic extreme. This concept of 'separateness' and white superiority was implemented in law by the National Party, who came to power in 1948, promising support for poor Afrikaners.

The government enacted a Population Registration Act in 1950 to slot all citizens into an appropriate race group, and to outlaw interracial marriage and sexual relations. The Group Areas Act (1950) divided every town into defined sectors where only members of particular groups could own or occupy property, requiring the removal of many Coloured and Asian households. Dr Hendrick Verwoerd, a chief promoter of apartheid legislation and prime minister from 1958, consolidated a policy to convert African reserves into 'independent homelands', another way to deprive citizens of access to political rights in the South African heartland.

Most resented of all were the 'pass laws', which restricted the movement of the African population. It is no surprise that the 1950s also saw a rise in resistance. While confrontations between campaigners and the authorities were initially non-violent, the tone was set to change following the massacre at Sharpeville *(see opposite)* and the subsequent banning of the ANC and PAC.

mentary minority in favour of neutrality, he led his country into the war against Nazi Germany. South African troops thus entered the fray in North Africa and Italy.

Although Smuts drafted the human rights declaration of the United Nations charter, South Africa was almost immediately under fire for its own human rights record and the country ended up pulling out of the UN agencies. Under pressure from the multi-racial Commonwealth, South Africa with-

Hector Pietersen, first victim of the riot police in Soweto, 1976

drew from its historical relationship with Britain, becoming an independent republic in 1961. Western nations imposed trade embargos, especially on military equipment.

Society Under Tension

In 1948, the all-white electorate voted out Smuts' United Party in favour of the National Party, whose rigidly segregationist policy of apartheid (*see box opposite*) led to South Africa becoming an international pariah.

Violent protests against apartheid, and the government's reaction, kept South Africa in the international spotlight. In 1960, opposition to the pass laws culminated in a demonstration at Sharpeville, in the Transvaal, when the police opened fire on the crowd, killing 69 blacks. In 1976, following a government decision to enforce the use of Afrikaans in schools, protests erupted in Soweto and spread to townships across the country. Over 600 were killed during this period of resistance and, in response, the government placed a ban on individuals and organisations suspected of subversion.

New unrest sweeping the townships during the mid-1980s prompted a state of emergency. Thousands, almost all blacks, were arrested and then held without trial. Violence dominated television screens abroad until news crews were finally barred.

Under growing internal and external pressures the government changed direction dramatically and decided to scrap much of the legal structure of apartheid. In 1990 President F.W. de Klerk legalised the African National Congress and other previously banned organisations, and released ANC leader Nelson Mandela after 27 historic years in prison.

Miracle of Democracy

The country's first all inclusive election, held in April 1994, was relayed round the world as a 'miracle of democracy'. Nelson Mandela came to power as president at the head of the ANC, in a government of national unity.

Voted back into power with a clear majority in the 1999 and 2004 elections, the ANC still has much prestige, although Mandela's successor, Thabo Mbeki, has faced tough challenges.

Mandela victorious in 1994

While major social and economic reform is the government's top priority, foreign investment has been slow to materialise, particularly discouraged by a rise in violent crime. But at last South Africa has a democratic constitution, allowing all its citizens to study, work and move freely in their own country. The world watches with hope as a crucial new era unfolds.

Historical Landmarks

c.8000BC San inhabit the southwestern regions of southern Africa.
From 200AD The semi-nomadic Khoikhoi begin farming the land.
1488 Bartolomeu Dias lands at Mossel Bay and sails round the Cape.
1652 Jan van Riebeeck sets up Dutch supply station at Table Bay.
1658 Slaves first brought to the Cape; first large-scale vineyard planted.
1795 The British annex the Cape. Territory is returned to the Dutch in 1803, but retaken in 1806 and ceded formally to Britain in 1814.
1820–8 Zulu king Shaka extends his territory, vanquishing other tribes.
1834 Slavery is abolished in all British territories.
1836–54 Voortrekkers travel northwards to escape British domination.
1838 Voortrekkers led by Andries Pretorious defeat Zulus at Blood River.
1852 British grant limited self-government to Boer republic of Transvaal.
1854 The Boer Independent Republic of the Orange Free State founded.
1867 Diamonds discovered at Kimberley.
1877 Britain annexes the Transvaal.
1879 British and Zulu forces clash; Zulus decisively defeated at Ulundi.
1880–1 The Transvaal declares itself a republic. First Anglo-Boer war.
1886 Gold discovered in the Transvaal; Johannesburg founded.
1899–1902 Second Anglo-Boer War, in which Boers are beaten.
1910 The Union of South Africa is established.
1913 Natives Land Act is passed, limiting land ownership for blacks.
1948 National Party under D.F. Malan elected; apartheid acts follow.
1952 The ANC launches the Defiance Campaign.
1960 Police shoot 69 demonstrators in Sharpeville.
1961 South Africa becomes a republic and leaves the Commonwealth.
1964 Following his arrest in 1962, Mandela is given a life sentence.
1976 Police violence in Soweto ignites resistance across country.
1984 Anglican Archbishop Desmond Tutu is awarded Nobel Peace Prize.
1990 President De Klerk begins to scrap apartheid; Mandela released.
1994 The first democratic election held; Mandela is first black President.
1999 Second democratic election returns ANC to power under Mbeki.
2004 Mbeki and the ANC win third election with 70 percent majority.

WHERE TO GO

The size of France, Germany, Holland and Belgium combined, South Africa is too big to get to know in a single visit, so in the following pages we set out the highlights to help you choose an itinerary.

As most international flights to South Africa land at Johannesburg, we too begin in this dynamic city, which is situated in the province of Gauteng. After a look at nearby Pretoria, with a diversion to the resort of Sun City, we head for Mpumalanga Province and South Africa's prime tourist attraction, the Kruger National Park. Crossing the mountains of KwaZulu-Natal, we come to bustling Durban on the Indian Ocean and take a trip north into Zululand. Then we jump to Port Elizabeth, following the coast clockwise along the Garden Route and all the way to Cape Town, which becomes a base for visits to the Cape of Good Hope and to the Cape wine country. Finally, the circle is completed by looking at various ways back to Johannesburg: the luxurious Blue Train; the long drive across the Great Karoo to Kimberley; or still further north to the fringes of the Kalahari Desert.

GAUTENG

Gauteng is a province that accounts for just 1.5 percent of South Africa's surface area, yet whose estimated 12 million residents represent a quarter of the national population and generate 40 percent of its GDP. The explanation for this unusual concentration of wealth and populace is simple – gold.

Most of the world's great cities were built on a river, but Johannesburg – Gauteng's bustling administrative capital – owes its existence to an underground stream of gold. The discovery

The stunning view from Cape Town's Table Mountain

of this rich seam in 1886 transformed the meagre grazing land above it into South Africa's biggest city in just three years.

Johannesburg

As southern Africa's transport hub, **Johannesburg** (popularly known as Jo'burg) is often considered to be merely a springboard for travel to other parts of South Africa or the continent. Nevertheless, it offers some of Africa's best nightlife, shopping and hotel opportunities. The city is at its best in summer (Nov–Mar); warm, sunny mornings may turn into stormy afternoons, but torrential rains soon move on, leaving the city refreshed.

Like every South African city, Johannesburg's population patterns remain influenced by the racial segregation laws enacted under apartheid. Some 50,000 Asians were resettled in their own suburb, Lenasia, and blacks were assigned to vast townships on the outskirts, such as Soweto and Alexandria.

The skyline of Johannesburg

City Centre

Downtown Johannesburg is a colourful mix of tall skyscrapers, small Indian bazaars and traditional African *muti* (medicine) shops, where smart-suited office workers rub shoulders with beggars and hawkers. It is also a noted crime hotspot, so don't wander around with an expensive camera, watch or pair of sunglasses, or more money than you actually need.

Some Jo'burgers out and about

Throughout the city centre a relaxation of restrictions on street trading has resulted in hundreds of hawkers setting up market stalls or simply spreading a cloth on the ground and selling every imaginable commodity. Africa has come to South Africa's financial hub.

Among all the office buildings it's hard to find many historical monuments, but local preservationists are proud of the red-brick **Rissik Street Post Office**, which was started in 1897 and adorned with a clock tower after the Anglo–Boer War.

Over in Bree Street is the Newtown Cultural Precinct, a former fruit and vegetable market. Here you will find the **MuseumAfrica** (open Tues–Sun 9am–5pm; admission fee; tel: 011-833 5624), with an excellent range of African historical and cultural exhibits. The other end of the long building houses the **Market Theatre** complex (tel: 011-832 1641, <www.markettheatre.co.za>), which nurtured a thriving protest theatre movement in the apartheid era.

To the west of the Newtown market, a big concrete shopping centre in vaguely Moghul style called **Oriental Plaza** stretches from Bree Street to Main Street. The smell of spices greets you before you arrive. Connecting courtyards are ringed by Indian restaurants, snack bars and shops.

Housed in a building designed by Sir Edwin Lutyens, the **Johannesburg Art Gallery** (open Tues–Sun 10am–5pm; free; guided tours available; tel: 011-725 3130) is set in **Joubert Park**, the city's oldest park. The collection concentrates on the 19th and early 20th centuries, and includes a small but representative display of South African art. Bear in mind that the surrounding area is one of the worst spots for street crime.

Immediately northwest of the city centre, in Braamfontein, the **University of the Witwatersrand** is Africa's biggest English-language university. To the west of Wits is the modern campus of Rand Afrikaans University.

North of the city centre, the modest but pleasant **Johannesburg Zoo** (open daily 8.30am–5.30pm; tel: 011-646 2000;

Enjoying a *braai* (barbecue) in Soweto

admission fee) lies in Rosebank, also known for its shopping malls and occasional art displays at Zoo Lake on Sundays. The nearby suburbs of Norwood and Melville are a good choice for eating out and, further north, fashionable **Sandton** has some excellent hotels and a vast shopping complex.

Soweto

An organised day tour of **Soweto** (a contraction of South Western Townships) can be arranged through any hotel and makes a striking contrast to hanging out in the prosperous northern suburbs. Tours pass through various neighbourhoods, most poor and cramped, except the exclusive street known as Millionaires' Row.

The site of No. 14 Shaft of Crown Mines in Alamein Road, southwest of the city centre, is the focus of **Gold Reef City** (open Tues–Sun; admission fee; tel: 011-496 1600), a theme park with fairground rides, shows, bars and a decent hotel, all in the style of the 1890s, as well as restaurants and shops. The highlight is a trip through an authentic gold mine. Wearing protective gear and miners' lamps, visitors descend 220m (722ft) below ground. Every Sunday, local miners don skins and feathers to perform the *Isicathulu*, or 'Gumboot' dance.

> Johannesburg grew from the diggers' camps that proliferated following the discovery of gold in 1886. Since that time, the gold mining industry has been the backbone of South Africa's economy. Miners face tough working conditions – even though refrigerated air is constantly pumped through the networks of narrow shafts, air temperatures often exceed 32ºC (90ºF).

Next to the Gold Reef complex is the **Museum of Apartheid** (open Tues–Sun 10am–5pm; unsuitable for young children; tel: 011-496 1822), with graphic displays relating to the grim history of apartheid and the perils of racial discrimination.

Recently proclaimed a UNESCO World Heritage Site, the **Sterkfontein Caves** (open Tues–Sun, guided tours every 30 minutes; admission fee; tel: 011-956 6342), west of Johannesburg, have yielded more than 500 hominid fossils, most famously a 2.5 million year old skull discovered in 1936 and nicknamed 'Mrs Ples' (short for *Plesianthropus transvaalensus*, though the skull is now assigned to the species *Australopithecus Africanus*, and thought to be male). Unearthed in 1998, a near-complete skeleton dating back 3.5 million years is the oldest hominid fossil known from southern Africa.

Pretoria (Tshwane)

In the spring (October and November) the garden city of **Pretoria** shimmers in a purple bloom of 60,000 jacaranda trees, originally introduced to South Africa from Brazil. You'll find Pretoria an agreeable place at any time, though, with beautiful parks and some innovative architecture.

Tshwane, the recently adopted name for the Greater Pretoria metropolitan area, has a population in excess of 1 million. As the administrative capital of South Africa, the city itself supported an unusually high proportion of whites during the apartheid era, many of whom were government employees. Although Pretoria remains the joint capital in the new South Africa, the government and civil service is no longer dominated by whites, and the city has largely shed its negative image as the conservative heartland of the apartheid administration.

Pretoria's historic heart is **Church Square**, where early settlers built their first church in the 1850s. A statue of Paul Kruger – the craggy patriarch who was elected president of the Transvaal Republic four times in the late 19th century – stands in the middle of the square. Around the base of the monument are statues of four citizen-soldiers of the era. Photographers equipped with instant cameras stake out this spot, waiting to snap tourists then sell them the photos.

Some distinguished official buildings from earlier days face the square: the old **Raadsaal** (parliament), in Italian Renaissance style; the old **South African Reserve Bank**, designed by Sir Herbert Baker; and the **Palace of Justice**, used as a hospital during the British occupation of 1900. Among the modern buildings near the square that lift the skyline is the **Volkskas Centre**, headquarters of the first Afrikaner-controlled bank.

Strijdom Square, located just down the street from the Volkskas skyscraper, honours J.G. Strijdom, prime minister in the 1950s, with a bust that is about 12 times life size. Adjoining the square is the **State Theatre complex**, which comprises six auditoria and may be viewed on guided tours (tel: 012-322 1665, <www.statetheatre.co.za>). A couple of blocks away up Van der Walt Street, a huge municipal office building, the Munitoria, contains the Information Bureau, which hands out local maps, leaflets and advice.

Pretoria – the Jacaranda City

Pretoria's Union Buildings

If you really can't manage a trip to a game park, you might look in at Pretoria's **National Zoological Gardens** (open daily 8am–5pm; admission fee; tel: 012-328 3265), with around 3,500 species displayed in showy flower gardens; a cable car is suspended above some areas. Next door, the **National Cultural History and Open Air Museum** (open daily 8am–4pm; admission fee) has something for everyone, from Stone Age rock engravings to a replica of General Smuts' bedroom. On show are old wagons and cannon and a room full of historic bibles. The hoard of 18th-century silver bowls, pots and pitchers from the Cape Colony is one of the best in the nation.

Sir Herbert Baker designed Pretoria's noblest architectural ensemble, the **Union Buildings**, a couple of mirror-image structures linked by a semi-circular colonnade. This big ministerial complex, the site of President Mandela's inauguration in 1994, looks down on formal gardens (open Mon–Fri; admission fee; tel: 012-325 2000) of brilliant flowers, sculpted trees and flawless lawns.

Bird-watchers don't know which way to turn in South Africa, where even suburban gardens harbour the most exotic birds in wild colour schemes. For a rapid initiation try the **Transvaal Museum** (open Mon–Sat 9am–5pm, Sun 11am–5pm; admission fee; tel: 012-322 7632) in Paul Kruger Street, where every species of South African bird is identified. Among other educational devices, there is a sort of jukebox for birdcalls. As a national research organisation, the museum also covers butterflies, reptiles and other aspects of natural history.

South of Pretoria

To the south of the city in the Fountains Valley Nature Reserve, a military stronghold built in 1898, commands strategic views of both Pretoria and the fertile countryside around. **Fort Klapperkop** has been spruced up and now serves as a museum of the military history of the Zuid-Afrikaansche Republiek, the Transvaal republic of the 19th century.

For miles around Pretoria, the hilltop **Voortrekker Monument** (open daily 9am–4.45pm; admission fee; tel: 012-326 6770) stands out. The looming structure was built as a shrine dedicated to the fortitude of the pioneers of the 1830s who trekked from the Cape to the Transvaal to perpetuate their language, religion and way of life.

Sun City

South Africa's answer to Las Vegas lies 90 minutes' drive west of Johannesburg, on the fringes of the Kalahari. During the late 1970s, the austere restrictions in South Africa encouraged businessman Sol Kerzner to create an escape valve in what was then the homeland of Bophuthatswana. Today, Sun City is part of the North West Province of South Africa and the resort's hedonistic pleasures are geared towards the family as much as the gambler.

Rising like a mirage from the dusty bushveld, this glitzy resort contains casinos, cinemas, restaurants and numerous hotels. The extraordinary Lost City complex is the biggest such project ever achieved in Africa and features a spectacular five-star hotel *(see page 128)*, complete with artificial beach and wave pool. Outdoor facilities include a world-class golf course and an artificial lake for waterskiing and parasailing. Nearby is Pilanesberg National Park *(see page 35)*.

Buses run frequently to Sun City from the Rotunda at Johannesburg's railway station and many tour companies operate excursions for a day or longer. For resort details visit <www.suninternational.com>.

Inside the granite monument a sculpted frieze commemorates incidents that took place during the treks. The monument's museum houses the Voortrekker Tapestry, a series of vivid needlework panels depicting events of the Great Trek. The museum also has dioramas that illustrate pioneer life; the typical Boer living room might be mistaken for an old Dutch farm scene were it not for the lion skin on the floor.

Further Afield

Forty kilometres (25 miles) east of Pretoria, at **Cullinan**, is the Premier Diamond Mine, a historic site in its own right: the 3,106-carat Cullinan diamond was unearthed here in 1905. From the fist-sized stone were hewn the Star of Africa and other gems now among the British Crown Jewels. The mine is still in business, producing about a million carats a year, though most of the stones are used for industrial purposes. Tour operators in Johannesburg and Pretoria run excursions to the mine, or you can go by car. The workings can be visited each weekday morning (you'll need strong shoes). Back in Johannesburg you can follow up the story by watching diamonds being cut and set into jewellery.

Well known for their colourful geometric wall-paintings, the Ndebele people derive from the Nguni of KwaZulu-Natal. Those found to the north of Pretoria are the southern Ndebele, whose homeland of KwaNdebele was established in 1984. Ndebele people are also found in Zimbabwe.

The **Hartbeespoort Dam**, 35km (22 miles) west of Pretoria, in a beautiful location against the backdrop of the Magaliesberg Mountains, is the setting for numerous small holiday resorts, as well as a good snake park. The **De Wildt Cheetah Research Station**, off the R513 near the dam (open Tues, Thur, Sat and Sun 8.30am–noon and 2–6.30pm; tours by advance booking only; tel: 012-504 1921) is the first place where the cheetah was successfully bred in captivity.

Situated 40km (25 miles) northwest of Pretoria, the **Tswain Crater Museum** (open daily 9am–4pm; admission fee; tel: 012-790 2303) protects a 1.4-km (nearly 1-mile) wide meteorite crater and the brackish lake on its floor. A neighbouring cultural village is a good place to see the colourful geometric house paintings for which the Ndebele people are renowned.

A Ndebele child

About two hours' drive northwest of Pretoria, the 500 sq km (195 sq mile) **Pilanesberg National Park** (tel: 014-555 6135/6) consists of a scenic collapsed caldera where lion, elephant and rhino roam freely alongside various antelope and 350 bird species. Good internal roads and a wide range of accommodation options from campsites to the luxury Sun City complex make Pilanesberg ideal for a short self-drive safari out of Gauteng.

A more exclusive game-viewing experience is offered at **Madikwe Game Reserve** (access to overnight visitors only) on the Great Marico River on the Botswana border, where a similar range of species can be seen on guided game drives out of a few small and relatively costly lodges. Like the Pilanesberg, Madikwe has one definite advantage over the Kruger Park and environs, namely that it is free of malaria.

One of many striking views of the Blyde River Canyon in Mpumalanga

MPUMALANGA AND LIMPOPO

East of Gauteng, the sun-bleached highveld rolls on to a mighty escarpment, which plunges down to subtropical valleys below. This mountain region is one of South Africa's favourite holiday retreats, particularly as a stopover en route to or from the splendid game reserves of the north.

From Pretoria or Johannesburg to the Kruger National Park is about 400km (248 miles) on excellent roads. The trip eastwards starts in the grassy plains of the highveld but, less than halfway, the scenery dramatically changes. One minute you could be in Scotland, the next the hills are as rugged as those in North Dakota, then suddenly the road plunges from cool spruce forests to banana plantations on the hot, humid lowveld.

On the Road to Kruger

If you're in a hurry, you can fly to the Kruger National Park or one of the private reserves. Travellers less worried about time can drive or take coach tours, going out and back on Route N4. If you have a day or two to spare, though, it's more interesting to take one route to Kruger, travel through the park, leave by another gate and return to Gauteng on a different road, taking in some of the following highlights of Mpumalanga and Limpopo provinces.

Nelspruit, on the N4 and the Crocodile River, is the centre of a rich fruit-growing area which is surrounded by orange groves as well as orchards of mangoes, avocados and lichees. The town itself is handsome, with a population of more than 150,000.

An alternative route to the Kruger Park goes through the town of **Lydenburg**, where a few early buildings survive from the 1850s, and over **Long Tom Pass** to **Sabie**, the site of a rich seam of gold, now worked out. Long Tom Pass is named after a gun used by the Boers against the British in 1900; the scenery is striking for its scale and emptiness.

Pilgrim's Rest, in a valley to the north, is well worth a diversion. Amid delightful pastoral scenery the heavily gouged hillsides give a clue to the past. A prospector named Alec 'Wheelbarrow' Patterson first panned gold here in 1873. News of the easy pickings spread quickly and Pilgrim's Rest took on all the trappings of a gold rush – 18 pubs could hardly cope with the crowds of miners. In the 20th century, as the mining technology became more and more sophisticated, the gold effectively ran out in 1972. When operations were closed down the provincial authorities bought up the

Pilgrim's Rest

town and preserved it as an oasis of nostalgia, with museums, gold-panning demonstrations, shops and hotels.

The forestry centre of nearby **Graskop** is a small town with mini-markets where you can replenish your picnic supplies. Past the regional centre of **Hazyview**, the road leads to the Paul Kruger Gate of the Kruger National Park.

The Panorama Route

If you can take a little more time, try to work out a route that allows you to see the **Blyde River Canyon**. 'Awe-inspiring' is no exaggeration for the views in this part of the world, where the Drakensberg Mountains mark the transition from highveld to low. The geological surprises of the escarpment include rock faces weirdly coloured by minerals, lichens and algae. The gorge itself is visible from many lookout points that are reached by long or short walks from the road.

A view from the bridge at Bourke's Luck Potholes

Three sandstone peaks – round outcrops topped by grass-covered cupolas – are called the **Three Rondavels**. Beyond them, **Mariepskop** is a mountain that has been squared off like an aircraft carrier. Hillsides plunge to the river as it zigzags through the creases, widening at last behind the Blyde River Dam.

Visitors to **God's Window** are rewarded by a panoramic view of the lowveld. Near Bourke's Luck, named after an old gold mine, the rivers Blyde ('joyful') and Treur ('sorrowful') converge in a three-way gorge. Three aluminium bridges offer views of this natural drama, from thundering waterfalls to **Bourke's Luck Potholes**, which seem to have been excavated by some gigantic ice-cream scoop. Displays at a visitor centre explain the local natural history. Accommodation is available at the **Aventura Blydepoort Resort** (tel: 013-769 8005).

KRUGER NATIONAL PARK

Close to 2 million hectares in size, the **Kruger National Park** ◄ (park gates open 5.30am–6.30pm in summer; 6.30am–5.30pm in winter; admission fee) is South Africa's biggest wildlife sanctuary. It contains more mammal species than any other game reserve in Africa, with the exception of Kafue National Park in Zambia. At least 10,000 elephant are resident within its boundaries, together with an estimated 25,000 buffalo, 120,000 impala and 30,000 zebra. And close to half a million humans clock in each year.

In recent years, most of the non-hunting reserves in the eastern lowveld have removed their fences bordering the Kruger National Park, so that wildlife can move freely between. The Kruger Park now also forms the core of

Before arriving in the area, don't forget to start taking anti-malaria pills, since both the Kruger Park and the private reserves alongside it are in a malaria zone (see page 114).

the Great Limpopo Trans-frontier Park, which – following full amalgamation with Zimbabwe's Gonarezhou National Park and Mozambique's Limpopo National Park – will probably rank as Africa's largest game reserve with an area of 35,000 sq km (22,000 sq miles).

Predicting the weather for this vast park is tricky, but the rainy season extends from September or October to March or April – mostly as brief thunder showers.

Accommodation

A place to stay may be reserved up to a year in advance through a travel agency or by writing to the SANParks, PO Box 787, Pretoria 0001. If you leave it to the last minute, you still stand a chance if you call the reservation service (tel: 012-428 9111). You can also use SANParks website for information and bookings at <www.sanparks.org>.

If no space is available, you might consider joining a package tour, as the tour operators make block bookings; or you could try to find accommodation in a hotel or camping ground outside the park but near enough for you to go in for day trips.

There are 18 rest camps, mostly in the park's southern half, where visitor traffic is concentrated. Those listed below have a restaurant, shop, petrol station and varied accommodation:

Berg-en-dal. An upmarket, modern camp set in hilly landscape overlooking the Matjulu Dam. Its well-fenced grounds are one of the few places where you can walk in the park.

Lower Sabie. A relatively small camp set attractively on the banks of a dam on the Sabie River in a prime viewing area.

Olifants. As the name suggests, this camp is in elephant country, set on a clifftop above the Olifants River, haunt of hippos. The surrounding roads offer reliable game viewing.

Shingwedzi. One of the newer camps, set attractively on the stretch of the eponymous river above the Kanniedood Dam.

Skukuza. More beds than any other camp and also more facilities, including a bank, post office and a car hire agency. It also lies at the heart of some of the best game-viewing roads.

Kruger offers the chance to see the world's largest land mammal

A square-lipped trio

On the Lookout

Unless you pay attention you could spend hours roaming the park and see nothing more glamorous than antelope. Keep your eyes shifting from near to far, peering into the shadows, alert for any movement or discrepancy. Pay special attention to waterholes and rivers, as the largest concentrations of animals are seen in these places. Remember it's best to drive at well below the 50km/h (31mph) limit – especially on dirt roads, where there is more dust to stir up *(see page 110)*.

In the African summer the best times for spotting game are from sunrise to perhaps 11am and again in the late afternoon in the hour before the park and camp gates close. In the cooler season the waterholes are active from predawn to noon and game can be seen at any time of day, though predators remain most active in the early morning and late afternoon.

Wilderness Trails

Perhaps the irony has struck you: in game parks it's the humans who are confined – to camps and cars. In the Kruger, the way to escape this restriction is to join a Wilderness Trail group – eight hardy trekkers accompanied by an armed tracker and ranger. The trail followers, travelling on foot, stay out in the bush for three nights. Only small numbers of visitors (aged 12 to 60) can be accepted. Reservations can be made one year in advance, or you can always try for a last-minute cancellation (tel: 012-428 9111 for information).

The Residents of Kruger Park

Antelope. A generic term for ungulates from the wildebeest to the tiny steenbok. Of the 21 species here, the most common are impala.

Baboon. A troop of baboons is held in line by the big, dominant males, who grow to weigh nearly 41kg (90lbs) and can live to the age of 45.

Birds. Of the park's 510 species, several are rare outside of protected areas, including the ground hornbill, saddle-billed stork and kori bustard.

Buffalo. Africa's only species of wild cattle, these heavily built animals stay close to waterholes or rivers, and tend to be more active at night.

Cheetah. This sleek spotted cat hunts its prey in broad daylight, reaching speeds of more than 100km/h (62mph) in short bursts.

Elephant. The largest land mammal, the African elephant can weigh as much as 6,300kg (6 tons). Females roam in loose-knit herds; males leave around age 12, drifting between herds or forming bachelor groups.

Giraffe. The world's tallest animal, male giraffes can grow to 5.5m (18ft). Vulnerable to attack by lions, they sleep briefly, standing up.

Hippopotamus. Weighing up to 2,000kg (2 tons), hippos lack sweat glands and submerge themselves by day to keep cool, grazing at dusk.

Spotted hyena. This alleged scavenger is also an efficient hunter. Clans of 10–100, led by a dominant female, are active mainly at night.

Leopard. A secretive nocturnal hunter, the leopard is hard to spot. It can usually be found along rivers, among rocky outcrops, behind foliage, or up trees, where it will often haul its kill to dine in comparative safety.

Lion. Outnumbering the maned males, lionesses do most of the hunting, but a hungry male will drive off the rest of the group at feeding time.

Rhinoceros. Poaching for horns has all but wiped out South African rhino herds. Kruger Park is one of the last major strongholds of this endangered species. There are two kinds of rhino: the square-lipped, or 'white', and the hook-lipped, or 'black', which is the more aggressive.

Zebra. Numbering about 30,000 in the Kruger Park, this timid creature feeds on grass alone, migrating often in search of new fields.

Private Game Parks

Another way to get close to nature – more comfortable but more expensive – is to book in at a **private game park**. Several operate in the bushveld along the western border of Kruger Park. Two- to five-day packages are offered, which include flights from Johannesburg to the airstrips at Phalaborwa or Skukuza (or to one of the reserves that has its own strip).

In a private reserve, transport is by open Land Rover, with expert rangers and trackers as guides. Vehicles are linked by radio, so word can be spread when rare animals are sighted. You can do more succesful spotting in the hours around dawn and dusk than you can in the national parks, and night safaris with spotlights reveal the nocturnal creatures you might never otherwise see. By day, rangers and trackers lead walks, while teaching you some of the secrets of the bush.

Luxury lodges, such as **MalaMala**, **Sabi Sabi** and **Londolozi** *(see pages 129–30)*, cosset their guests with the most attentive service and haute cuisine. Several other private establishments are somewhat less expensive but nevertheless provide expert rangers, air-conditioned accommodation, good food and swimming pools. Among a dozen or so in this group are **Thornybush** and **Inyati**. Information on accommodation in the private reserves, as well as in the national parks, is given in a brochure published by South African Tourism *(see pages 102 and 123)*.

Lions are the largest of Africa's three big cats

Hiking in Royal Natal National Park

KWAZULU-NATAL

KwaZulu-Natal province makes up only 8 percent of the nation's territory, but therein lies a remarkable geographical diversity, ranging from snow-prone mountains to a selection of beaches on the warm Indian Ocean. The people, too, range from Anglo to Zulu.

Vasco da Gama, the Portuguese navigator, first sighted these shores on Christmas Day in 1497 – hence the province's original name, 'Natal', Portuguese for Christmas. Following the political changes of April 1994 the province was renamed KwaZulu-Natal. It's capital is Pietermaritzburg, but its largest city is the Port of Durban.

Drakensburg Mountains

The provincial conservation authority, KZN Wildlife, is responsible for about 60 reserves and parks, which it keeps as unspoiled as possible while providing comfortable cottages and chalets and plenty of attractive campgrounds. Some of the most impressive reserves are in the **Drakensberg Mountains** in the west along the frontier with the Kingdom of Lesotho. Stone Age Bushmen were attracted here because of the availability of small game and fresh water. They were driven out by a succession of tribes, most recently the Ngwaneni, who today live within sight of the Drakensberg peaks in their traditional wattle huts, shaped like haystacks.

Proclaimed a UNESCO World Heritage Site in 2000, the KwaZulu-Natal part of this vast mountain range has long been protected within a series of conservation areas, most famously the Royal Natal National Park, the Giant's Castle Game Reserve, and the Kamberg and Loteni Nature Reserves. Extending over a total area of 243,000 hectares (600,453 acres), these contiguous protected areas are now collectively referred to as the **uKhahlamba-Drakensberg Park**, a combination of the Zulu and Afrikaans names for the spine-like range, which translate respectively as 'Barrier Of Spears' and 'Dragon's Mountains'.

A geological phenomenon known as the **Amphitheatre** constitutes the climax to the **Royal Natal National Park**. The panorama looks as if Mount Rushmore had been placed atop alpine foothills; the cliffs shoot down to steep green slopes. For mountain climbers, the highest peak, Mont-Aux-Sources, is a two-day undertaking: 3,282m (10,765ft) above sea level and 45km (28 miles) of difficult climbing, with some stupendous views as a reward. Mont-Aux-Sources is also accessible from the Free State if you go by Qwa Qwa.

The inhabitants of Royal Natal National Park include several species of mountain antelope, as well as large colonies of baboons and dassies (rock-climbing mammals that look like oversized guinea pigs). Bird-watchers have counted nearly 200 species. For nature-lovers of all kinds there are hiking trails and easy walks through enthralling scenery.

The **Giant's Castle Game Reserve**, another Drakensberg wilderness, contains fantastic rock formations, along with caves and various treasures of Bushman rock art. The 'castle' itself, a few feet higher than Mont-Aux-Sources, is so awe-inspiring that the Africans called it 'The Mountain Not To Point At'. Wildlife includes eland (the biggest antelope) and a giant vulture, the lammergeyer. Storm clouds gather in these mountains on most summer afternoons.

It's all downhill, slowly, from Giant's Castle to the coast. About halfway, at a refreshing altitude of 1,000m (3,280ft), is the resort centre of **Howick**. On the edge of town, the **Howick Falls**, plunging from street level into an abyss in the Umgeni Valley Nature Reserve, is a national monument.

How it falls in Howick

Pietermaritzburg

Some 24km (15 miles) southeast of Howick is **Pietermaritzburg**, the provincial capital, which is named after two Voortrekker leaders, Piet Retief and Gerrit Maritz. The name is routinely shortened to Maritzburg. A city of parks and gardens with a population of about 200,000, it's at its best in spring when the azaleas are in bloom.

The founders of 1838 built wide streets and Cape Dutch houses, but their dreams of an unfettered Boer culture soon came to an end; the British occupied the town in 1842.

Pietermaritzburg City Hall

Pioneer mementos, such as rifles, kitchen implements and a case full of *kappies* (bonnets), are displayed in the **Voortrekker Museum** (open Mon–Fri 9am–4pm, Sat 9am–1pm; admission fee; tel: 033-394 6834). A low building in Cape style, which dates from the year 1840, it began its existence as the Church of the Vow, built after the Battle of Blood River. Next door is the restored home of the Voortrekker hero, Andries Pretorius.

The fine Victorian **City Hall** (1893) is claimed to be the largest all-brick building south of the equator. Little shops and law offices line the narrow alleys nearby, whose names – like Chancery Lane and Gray's Inn Lane – evoke London's Inns of Court. This area was the financial district, too, until the local stock exchange went out of business in the depression of 1931.

The N3 from Pietermaritzburg to Durban, one of South Africa's best highways, passes through subtropical countryside that becomes ever more lush towards the coast. About halfway to the coast the motorway skirts the spectacular **Valley of a Thousand Hills**, through which the short but powerful Umgeni River journeys to the Indian Ocean. This is the same river that was last seen taking a shortcut at Howick Falls.

This is Zulu country and one of the tourist attractions is the **Phe-Zulu tribal kraal**, a 'living museum' (tel: 031-777 1208; coach parties from Durban). Each 'beehive' hut is designed to illustrate an aspect of tribal life. A highlight is the dancing display to the rhythm of a drum and two-toned string instruments.

Durban

They come from all parts of South Africa to hit the beaches and ride the surf or the roller coaster at **Durban** and, somehow, the town succeeds in combining the roles of brash beach resort and the busiest port in Africa.

Durban has come a long way since 1824, when a small British trading post was set up here to barter with the powerful Zulu nation. Originally called Port Natal, the settlement was renamed in 1835 in honour of the Governor of Cape Colony, General Sir Benjamin D'Urban. Despite many vicissitudes, the province of KwaZulu-Natal is the only one where the English language is more widely spoken than Afrikaans.

The personality of Durban is enlivened by its unique population mix: more than 800,000 Indian, 320,000 white and at least 2 million black (mostly Zulu) and Coloured people. As everywhere else in South Africa, the races live to a

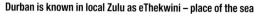

Durban is known in local Zulu as eThekwini – place of the sea

great extent in separate areas, they are close enough together to promote something of a cosmopolitan air. Even the black townships are relatively handy to the centre of town.

For the tourist, the centre of Durban is the beach. Along the city's **Golden Mile** run – from south to north – uShaka, Addington, South, North and Battery beaches. Closest to the business district, South Beach is usually the most crowded. **North Beach** is the hangout of surfers, with long, rolling waves and a comfortable sea temperature.

For those interested in marine wildlife, a certain highlight of Durban's seafront will be **uShaka Marine World** (open daily 9am–6pm; admission fee; <www.ushakamarineworld.co.za>). The Sea World zone features an aquarium built into a 1920s cargo steamer, with a large collection of live sharks. There are also daily shows featuring performing dolphins, seals and penguins, and, if you're brave enough, a shark dive tank.

The coast at Durban is the perfect place to catch a wave

Lined up on **Marine Parade** are the last surviving rickshaws in Durban. Transplanted here from Japan in Victorian times, the rickshaw quickly became a popular conveyance. Only a handful are left, pulled by Zulus in colourful tribal regalia.

Harbour tours and deep-sea cruises depart from the Victoria Embankment, which faces south across Durban Bay. The busy deepwater port

> Mohandas K. Gandhi, campaigner for Indian independence, first came to Durban in 1893 as a young lawyer and lived here on and off for 21 years, suffering many indignities because of his race. Gandhi conceived his philosophy of non-violent defiance in South Africa, where he led mass protests against discriminatory laws.

– which handles three times the tonnage of Cape Town, South Africa's second biggest port – makes for an interesting outing.

The business district is just a few steps inland from the Victoria Embankment. The **City Hall** is said to be a copy of Belfast's – plus palm trees on either side of the portico. It houses the Public Library, **Durban Art Gallery** (open daily; free) and the **Natural Science Museum** (open Mon–Sat 8.30am–4pm, Sun 11am–4pm; admission fee; tel: 031-311 2256). In nearby Smith Street the **Natal Playhouse** complex houses venues for the performing arts. At the **General Post Office** a plaque commemorates the arrival in Durban, just before Christmas 1899, of the young Winston Churchill after his escape from a Boer prisoner-of-war camp in Pretoria.

The heart of Durban's Indian business district, **Grey Street**, is a lively, exotic area to explore. Although only about 20 percent of the local Indian population is Muslim, the Juma Mosque on Grey Street is reputed to be the biggest mosque in the southern hemisphere. Its arcades are occupied by shops selling a range of delicacies and jewellery, saris (spelt *sarries* in Durban) and European fashions.

Nearby in Russell Street, the vast Indian Market (officially the **Victoria Street Market**) offers a sample of the East. Engaging salesmen all but persuade you to buy enough 'hell-fire curry powder' for life. Also on sale are Hindu religious pictures and coral and wood carvings, many of them imported.

For a further feel of the tropics, try the Durban **Botanic Gardens** (open daily; free) in Sydenham Road. In the orchid house there's a display of orchids, tropical ferns and vines. Outside, acres of lawns are shaded by an incredible variety of trees and elsewhere on the grounds there's a scent garden for the blind. Durban is proud of its parks, which include the formal **Japanese Gardens** and **Jameson Park**, where 200 varieties of roses bloom in springtime (September and October).

Golden beaches stretch in endless vistas north and south of Durban. To reach the south coast resorts you have to travel through the port and industrial areas. Sweeping sugar lands eventually materialise (some plantations and factories offer tours), followed by lush vegetation and uncrowded beaches.

North from Durban, the highway parallels the Indian Ocean between sugar plantations and the sea. The picturesque resort of **Umhlanga Rocks** (18km/11 miles from Durban), with a lighthouse on the beach, is one place where the bathing should be safe – it's the home of the Natal Sharks Board *(see page 56).*

Zululand

North of Durban, the part of KwaZulu-Natal known informally as **Zululand** offers some of the country's best game viewing in an excellent network of provincial and private reserves well suited to self-drive visitors. Other attractions include some fine remote beaches and a number of sites relating to the Zulu monarchy, which originated in the region.

A useful base for exploring this region, **St Lucia Village** overlooks the eponymous 325 sq km (125 sq mile) wetland, which was recently accorded UNESCO World Heritage Site status as the largest estuarine system in Africa. Protected within the **Greater St Lucia Wetland Park** (tel: 035-590 1340), the estuary harbours 800 hippos (the largest population in the country) and a similarly impressive crocodile population, while a checklist of 500 bird species includes pelicans, flamingos, spoonbills, fish eagles and Caspian terns.

A short drive inland of St Lucia, the **Hluhluwe-Imfolozi Game Reserve** (tel: 035-562 0848 or 550 8476) was proclaimed as two separate entities in 1897, the joint second-oldest game reserves in Africa. Hluhluwe (pronounced shloo-shloo-ee) and Imfolozi (formerly Umfolozi) are now linked by a corridor of state-owned land to create a total area of roughly 1,000 sq km (390 sq miles) in which some 81 mammal species have been recorded, including elephant, lion, leopard, cheetah, hunting dog, giraffe, warthog, impala and the localised nyala antelope.

The wetland of St Lucia

Hluhluwe-Imfolozi is best known for its dense rhino populations. In the early 1930s, only about 15 white rhinos were left in southern Africa, but a breeding programme at this reserve succeeded in increasing the local population to 1,000, and exporting a further 4,000 of these magnificent animals to other parks. Today, a similar

Zulu herbalist at Shakaland

battle is underway to save its cousin, the black rhino, also common here. Imfolozi's celebrated Wilderness Trail, established in 1957, allows you to explore the region on foot in the company of an experienced armed ranger.

Elephant, rhino, leopard, giraffe and nyala are among the game that you may be able to spot in KZN Wildlife's 36,000-hectare (88,956-acre) **Mkhuze** (formerly Mkuzi) **Game Reserve** (tel: 035-573 9001), which borders the St Lucia Wetland Park to the east. Mkhuze is celebrated for its tropical birdlife, while photographers are attracted to the hides overlooking its waterholes. Another popular destination with bird-watchers is **Ndumo Game Reserve**, set further north on the border with Mozambique.

Part rundown farmland, part hunting concession before it was acquired by Conservation Corporation Africa (CC Africa) in 1991, the private **Phinda Resource Reserve** was subjected to an ambitious programme of reintroductions – lion, cheetah, elephant et al – to boost resident populations of leopard, nyala and other antelope. Phinda today provides an upmarket (and expensive) safari experience to compare with any in Africa. Less luxurious but cheaper is nearby **Zulu Nyala Lodge**.

At **Shakaland** (tel: 035-460 0912), a large lodge set about 14km (9 miles) north of Eshowe, one can enjoy a fascinating Zulu cultural programme for a day, or overnight in a local beehive-style hut with modern lights and plumbing. Two smaller lodges offer a broadly similar experience: **Kwa-**

Bhekithunga (tel: 035-460 0644) is a personalised family-run lodge founded some 25 years ago as a craft centre for the disabled, while **Simunye** (tel: 035-450 3111) is an intimate riverside lodge that caters to overnight visitors only.

An important historical site near Ulundi is **Umgungundlovu**, former capital of King Dingane and burial place of the Voortrekker Piet Retief. Also close to Ulundi, the **Ondoni Cultural Museum** (open daily; admission fee; tel: 035-870 2051) is an on-site reconstruction of the capital founded by King Cetshwayo in 1873 and razed six years later by British troops in the last battle of the Anglo-Zulu War. The museum offers a low-budget version of the Shakaland experience, complete with affordable accommodation in beehive huts.

Farther inland you can visit two other **battlefields** of the 1879 Zulu War: Isandhlwana, where a British force was wiped

The Zulus

Numbering approximately 5 million, Zulus are the largest ethnic African group in South Africa. Once a mighty military power, they famously came into conflict with the Voortrekkers and the British Army in the 19th century. Having often been crudely stereotyped as cattle-herding peasants or bloodthirsty, spear-wielding tribalists, today most view themselves first and foremost as citizens of South Africa. While some live in rural areas of KwaZulu-Natal, where Zulu chiefs play a major role and the cult of the warrior is still prevalent, others are opting for an urban lifestyle, living in suburban areas with middle class jobs, while other, poorer city dwellers live in the townships.

Not all urban Zulus have turned away from their tribal heritage, and many remain faithful to traditional customs, such as a belief in ancestral spirits. And, in post-apartheid South Africa, there is official support for all aspects of Zulu culture from music and theatre to faith healing, with cultural villages established to promote indigenous crafts and customs.

out; and **Rorke's Drift**, the famous site where a British garrison held out against the Zulus. History buffs can spend weeks tracing the sites, where the Voortrekkers parlayed or fought with the Zulus, and following the progress of the Anglo–Boer War from the British disasters of 1899 and 1900 through their laborious advance and on to their eventual victory.

From Durban, if you are touring by car, you can head south by way of the coastal resorts and then through Transkei to East London. From there a transit of the Ciskei region brings you to Grahamstown and Port Elizabeth. Some tour companies offer trips inland to visit game and nature reserves, where you can hunt, hike or watch the wildlife. Alternatively, you can tour on your own. Malarial precautions are needed for some areas; contact the KwaZulu-Natal Tourism Authority *(see page 123)*.

Sharks

A single headline – 'Shark Attacks Swimmer!' – can turn a busy resort into a deserted village, so it's vital to protect the beaches from the deadly species that live in the Indian Ocean. The Natal Sharks Board catches over 1,000 sharks a year. Some 300 huge nets, spread at intervals along 320km (199 miles) of coastline in KwaZulu-Natal, protect 38 beaches.

Even so, the average beach in the province is closed to swimmers 20 days a year. The most dangerous season is from June to August, when sardines migrate close to the shore, attracting so many sharks that the nets are removed to avoid becoming clogged and damaged. The 'sardine run' is now marketed as an attraction in its own right. Those who call the Sardine Hotline (tel: 082-284 9495; June–July) can find out the exact location of sardine activity on the coast and attend the spectacle of shimmering shoals feasted upon by sharks, dolphins and gannets.

An audio-visual show and dissection is presented at the board's offices in the Durban resort of Umhlanga (Tues–Thurs 9am and 2pm, Sun 2pm; admission fee; <www.shark.co.za>).

Tsitsikama, Africa's first coastal national park *(see page 60)*

THE SOUTHERN COAST

South Africa's southern coast is a picturesque patchwork of beaches, forests and lakes. Inland attractions include the Addo Elephant Park, ostrich ranches and the Cango Caves.

Port Elizabeth

The country's motor industry is concentrated in **Port Elizabeth** (often called PE) and, perhaps fittingly, the centre of the city is violated by a network of elevated super-highways, isolating the business district from the harbour. But there is more to Port Elizabeth than first impressions suggest. About 2km (1½ miles) south of the city centre is **King's Beach**, popular with swimmers and surfers. Beyond, along Humewood Beach, the **Bayworld complex** (open daily 9am–5pm; dolphin presentations 11am and 3pm; admission fee; tel: 041-586 1051) features an excellent anthropological and natural history museum and an oceanarium, with an outstanding dolphin show.

Next door is Bayworld's snake park, where a seemingly carefree handler wraps himself in puff adders, cobras and mambas while reciting a speech on the art of avoiding snakebites. Some 400 species of plants flourish in the sultry Tropical House. In the Night House (just inside the door of the Tropical House) the hours are reversed, allowing you to see nocturnal animals active in the dim artificial light.

With a little imagination, you can picture Port Elizabeth as it must have been 60 years ago when the Campanile was built. The bell tower, 52m (171ft) tall and reminiscent of the one in Venice, rings out a 23-bell carillon concert every day at 8.32am and then at 1.32 and 6.02pm. You can climb it for a view over the city and harbour, but today the monument itself is almost invisible from the town, because of the motorway.

The **business district**, with big modern department stores, is what you'd expect in a city of more than half a million people. Main Street starts at the Mayor's Garden and the City Hall, a national monument dating from 1858. After a fire in 1977 the interior was re-done in a sparkling modern style, though no less stately than the building's exterior. A statue of Queen Victoria, facing the harbour, marks the main public library. A tourist office is also found here.

Roads inside Addo Elephant National Park pass near several water-holes where elephants are likely to appear in dry weather. Getting out of your car anywhere inside the enclosure is forbidden, except at designated lookout points, where visitors may exit their vehicle at their own risk. Another road along the outside has elevated viewing points. For more information visit <www.sanparks.org/parks/addo>.

Addo Elephant Park

An hour's drive from Port Elizabeth, the descendants of the last elephants to live wild in Cape Province thrive

➤ in the **Addo Elephant National Park**, which must surely rank as one of the best destinations in Africa for elephant watching. More than 400 remarkably relaxed pachyderms roam the park, while eight bull tuskers were recently relocated here from the Kruger National Park to broaden the gene pool. This was considerably reduced during the 1930s, when there were only six sexually active individuals.

During your visit, you might also glimpse black rhino, buffalo and several types of antelope. Restricting visibility, though, is the evergreen addo bush, which

Addo elephant and calf

is short but impenetrable. Among all the tangled creepers are beautiful midget trees – wonderfully bright when in flower.

The Addo elephants won world attention in the 1920s. Stalking valuable farm land, they terrified local residents and damaged crops. A famous hunter, Major Pretorius, was contracted to exterminate the herd. In a period of almost a year, he killed 120, but 15 of the most cunning elephants eluded him. Public sympathy subsequently welled up for the victims and the survivors were thus reprieved. Setting up a national park for them was easier than confining them. Various types of fencing were tried and failed, until a high fence of tram rails and steel cables was devised. Eventually, it will enclose most of the park's 7,735 hectares (19,105 acres).

The Garden Route

The N2 highway links Port Elizabeth and Cape Town. Composed of many kinds of landscape, exactly which stretch of this road deserves the semi-official title of the **Garden Route** is somewhat vague. The most attractive section of the route runs about 220km (137 miles) between the mouth of the Storms River and Mossel Bay.

Yellowwood in Tsitsikama

West from Port Elizabeth, **Jeffrey's Bay** is considered to be South Africa's surfing paradise, well known to members of the international surfing set, who arrive in March for the new season. All year round the immense pink arc of sand is a delight. The beach is also a treasure trove of seashells, as you'll see in the **shell museum** (open Mon–Sat 9am–4pm), located in the library on the seafront.

In majestic countryside to the west, a splendid national park is centred near the Storms River. An ingenious and graceful bridge with a span of 192m (630ft) offers a formidable view down the gorge to the river far below. On the landward side of the N2 is the **Tsitsikama National Park**, with trees such as yellowwood, stinkwood and candlewood. Hiking trails are laid out to provide surveys of the big trees, the ferns and lichen, and the wild flowers.

Across the highway the park continues for about 80km (50 miles) along the rugged shore. The first coastal national park on the continent of Africa, it's a sanctuary for otters, bushbacks and vervet monkeys, along with 210 species of birds. The restricted zone extends half a mile into the ocean, protecting dolphins, whales and the marine environment. The 41-km (25-mile) Otter Trail, leads hikers along the coastline over cliffs, through forests and across streams.

The Garden Route offers some sensational scenery: pine and eucalyptus trees stretch endlessly behind blossoming roadside trees; tortuous stretches of road pass through and over gorges; the ocean appears in sudden glimpses between sheer cliffs.

When the Portuguese navigators of the 15th century saw **Plettenberg Bay** they were moved to call it Bahia Formosa (Beautiful Bay) – a judgement today's traveller would find hard to disagree with. The vast, classic arc of sandy beach is a favourite with visitors from far and near. The cape that protects the bay, called Robberg (Seal Mountain), supports a nature reserve that's accessible on foot.

On the way from Plettenberg Bay to Knysna you may be startled to see a sign for the **Garden of Eden**. Here is a

The upmarket seaside resort of Plettenberg Bay

The Outeniqua Tjue-Chou

chance to sample the air of a primeval forest. The sun's rays are barely able to filter through interwoven branches of trees that were here long before the coast was first sighted. Many of the garden's trees have been labelled by the Forestry Department for educational purposes.

The Knysna forests cover 80,000 hectares (197,600 acres), and are as valuable as they are beautiful. They were badly diminished in the 19th and early 20th centuries by reckless exploitation. With timberland constituting barely one percent of South Africa's total area, this resource is now carefully controlled by the government.

The town of **Knysna** (the 'K' is silent) is a popular resort that possesses an intriguing history. It was founded by a gentleman named George Rex, who was widely believed to be an illegitimate son of King George III of England. After arriving from the Cape at the beginning of the 19th century, he bought a big farm along the Knysna lagoon and turned the district into a seaport and a shipbuilding and timber centre. Boats and furniture are still made in Knysna, although the port lost its commercial importance with the arrival of the railway. Enthusiasts should make sure they do not miss the **Outeniqua Tjue-Chou**, a steam train that still runs from Knysna to George.

The Heads, a famous rocky beauty spot, marks the dramatic entry of the Indian Ocean into Knysna's lagoon. The lagoon stretches far inland and provides ideal conditions for anglers and sailors alike. An unusual landmark along the lagoon is **Holy Trinity Church** at Belvidere, built in the 19th century along the lines of a Norman church. It's one of the smallest churches in South Africa, with enough room for only 65 people.

More lagoons, lakes, timberland and voluptuously moulded hills characterise the Garden Route west of Knysna. The next resort along the highway, **Wilderness**, is not as deserted as its name suggests, offering hotels, camping sites and caravan parks, although there are also miles of unspoiled beaches.

George, the regional centre located at the intersection of the Garden Route and a main road to the Little Karoo, was named after George Rex's putative father, King George. The most remarkable structure in this plateau town of 50,000 is an impressive **Dutch Reformed Church** – blindingly white and of dignified proportions.

The Little Karoo

In strangely beautiful semi-desert beyond the Outeniqua Mountains, about 56km (35 miles) inland from George, **Oudtshoorn** is the capital of the Little Karoo. A stroll along any shopping street will soon show you what's different about this place. The stores sell ostrich feathers of many colours, empty ostrich eggs, dried ostrich meat, ostrich-hide wallets – even lamps and ashtrays standing on ostrich feet. Ostriches are big business in Oudtshoorn.

The **ostrich ranches** on the outskirts of town offer

Ostrich racing in the Little Karoo

an inimitable experience. In their thousands, nature's mightiest birds strut and scratch or stand about with vacant expressions in their bulging eyes. Guided tours of the farms cover the history of the Little Karoo's 90,000-strong herd, the boom of the Victorian era when ostrich feathers sold for 500 rand per kg (2.2lbs) and even tell you how to hatch an ostrich egg. There are ostrich races, in which the fleet, muscular, earth-bound bird have to run with 'jockeys' on their backs.

Why Oudtshoorn? It seems ostriches are happiest in a hot, dry climate; they like the type of alfalfa grown here and the availability of their favourite diet supplements – sand, stones and insects. In the same area other farms raise crocodiles for their skins and angora rabbits for their fur.

Twenty-six km (16 miles) north of Oudtshoorn, in the foothills of the Swartberg (Black Mountain), is another popular attraction, the **Cango Caves** (open daily, hourly guided tours; admission fee; tel: 044-272 7410). They're easy to reach over a well-built mountain road that mostly follows a meandering river, its banks fringed by weeping willows. The caves once sheltered Bushmen, whose paintings were found on the entrance walls. Guides escort visitors into a series of chambers, pointing out the suggestive formations of stalactites and stalagmites. Modern amenities include refreshments and babysitters.

The Western Cape whale route is active from June to September, affording visitors incredible views of migrating whales. Sometimes the giant sea mammals have passed so close to shore that onlookers have been soaked by their mighty spray. A popular spot for whale watching is at Hermanus, where a 'whale crier' blows a horn to alert spectators.

The last resort on the seaside section of the Garden Route is **Mossel Bay**, a working seaport with some beaches and natural swimming

The road to Swellendam

pools among the rocks. Sailing ships visited the bay as early as 1488, when the Portuguese navigator Bartolomeu Dias became the first European to touch South African soil. The **Bartolomeu Dias Museum Complex** (open Mon–Fri 9am–5pm, Sat and Sun 9am–4pm; admission fee; tel: 044-691 1067), housed inside a converted granary, is dedicated to his memory. Displays include a full-scale replica of Dias' surprisingly small caravel. The first permanent settlement at Mossel Bay was established some 300 years later, although passing ships often stopped for water and to trade with the local Hottentots.

The road to Cape Town heads away from the coast to **Swellendam**, one of the Cape's first inland towns. It has a curious past – declared independence from the Dutch East Indies Company in 1795, only to submit to the British the year after. Some fine buildings date from the 18th century and the wool boom of the 19th century. Close by, **Bontebok National Park** is home to the rare bontebok and other antelopes.

Cape Town is surrounded by a breathtaking barrier of mountains

CAPE TOWN

One of the great experiences for any traveller is the first sight of **Cape Town's** classic combination of cloud-topped mountain, skyscrapered flatland and the Atlantic Ocean.

Even though the climate suits pines, palms and frangipani, and the winters are mild, the locals complain. After all, it rains a lot and, in summer, a southeasterly wind assails the city for days at a time. Called the Cape Doctor, it is credited with sweeping away germs, mosquitoes and air pollution. During this season, Table Mountain acquires its distinctive 'tablecloth' – a strip of cloud that hovers over the summit. The mountain itself is visible to ships as far as 160km (100 miles) off.

Cape Town's main street, **Adderley Street**, runs along the modern façade of the railway terminus. Between the station and the docks, the zone called the Foreshore has been reclaimed from the sea and is now occupied by an overpowering array of elevated highways and buildings. The pedestrian mall on St George's Street hosts traditional marimba dance displays at lunchtime and on Saturday morning.

The giant **Civic Centre** straddling Hertzog Boulevard houses municipal officials and also the **Nico Malan Opera House and Theatre**, whose up-to-date technology behind the scenes can be seen on interesting guided tours.

City Centre

Pedestrians make their way underground on the landward side of the railway station. In the passage beneath Strand Street the tourist information office offers maps and accommodation advice. There's also an old postal stone, under which 17th-century sailors put letters to be picked up by homeward-bound ships.

Trafalgar Place, off Adderley Street, is the site of Cape Town's outdoor flower market, run by women of the Malay community. The Cape Malays are mostly the descendants of slaves brought from Southeast Asia in the late 17th century. They are Muslims and some still live in the **Malay Quarter**, or **Bo-Kaap**, near the business district (beyond Buitengracht Street). It's worth a visit to see the pastel-coloured houses, steep cobbled streets and minarets. Here you will also find the Jamai (or Queen Victoria) Mosque, Cape Town's oldest, dating back to 1850. Muslims of Indian extraction also live in this district, which survived the relocations of the apartheid era. Ironically, the character of the Malay Quarter is now threatened by the end of residence restrictions, as well-heeled outsiders try to buy up property here.

Colourful Bo-Kaap

Most of Cape Town's inhabitants are Cape Coloured, that is, of mixed descent involving early white settlers, Hottentots and indigenous blacks or imported slaves. They outnumber the whites by nearly two to one. The black population of Cape Town is small, amounting to one out of every eight residents. Most of the blacks are Xhosa speakers; listen for the amazing clicking sounds in their conversation.

Cape Town **City Hall**, an Italian Renaissance-type palace from the early 20th century, faces the **Grand Parade**, once used as a parade ground for troops. Before that the Dutch East Indies Company's first building in the Cape stood on this spot – an earthwork fort of 1652. Now the Parade is a large car park, with a fruit and flower market and, every Wednesday and Saturday morning, a flea market. Beware of pickpockets here.

Beyond the Grand Parade stands the **Castle of Good Hope** (open daily 9am–5pm, except Christmas; admission fee; tel: 021-469 1084), the oldest building in South Africa, a sturdy, pentagonal fortress surrounded by a restored moat and inviting gardens. Guides lead tours of the castle several times a day, recounting its history, explaining the tactical layout and showing off the dungeons. The castle contains small military and maritime museums and also the William Fehr Collection of paintings, Cape silver and furniture and Asian porcelain.

Facing on to the cobbled **Greenmarket Square**, the **Old Town House** is a grand Baroque building dating from 1761 that served as the city hall until 1905. Now the white building with green shutters holds the Michaelis Collection of Dutch and Flemish art, including a treasured Frans Hals portrait and dozens of oils by his contemporaries. The **Groote Kerk** (Great Church), at the point where Adderley Street runs into pedestrianised Government Avenue, is sometimes called the oldest church in South Africa. Not much remains of the original Dutch Reformed church of the 17th century. The clock tower dates from 1703 and the rest was rebuilt much later.

Government Avenue, an oak-shaded gravel walk nearly a kilometre long, is a restful place to take a stroll in central Cape Town. It runs down the middle of the original Dutch East Indies Company's **Garden**, laid out by the first governor, Jan Van Riebeeck. Here, some 300 slaves produced fruit and vegetables for settlers and the visiting ships of the Company. About one-third of the original farm area has been turned into a resplendent botanical garden; the rest is occupied by buildings as important as the South African Houses of Parliament.

Several cultural institutions are sited around the Company's Garden, including the **South African National Gallery** (open Tues–Sun 10am–4.30pm, closed Easter and 1 May; free), which highlights the work of South African artists and also has a strong showing of English painters.

The Houses of Parliament

Nearby, the **Jewish Museum** (open Sun–Thur 10am–5pm, Fri until 2pm; closed Jewish holidays; admission fee) occupies the Greek-columned building of South Africa's first synagogue (1862); next door is the twin-towered Gardens Synagogue.

Dioramas of natural history and prehistoric life, plus a valuable collection of Bushmen rock paintings, are on show at the **South African Museum** (open daily 10am–5pm; tel: 021-481 3000), the oldest institution of this kind in the country.

Docks and Harbour

The port area starts close to the city centre, but it's so big you may want to explore it by car. Probably the best way to see the fleets of banana boats, fishing trawlers and container ships is on a harbour cruise or a trip round Table Bay.

The ambitious development scheme for the two oldest dock basins at the **Victoria & Alfred Waterfront** (tel: 021-408 7600, <www.waterfront.co.za>) has revitalised the area, creating a complex of restaurants, shops and entertainment centres, the South African Maritime Museum and a hotel in a former warehouse. The area has now become the Cape's biggest magnet for visitors, although it remains a busy working port.

A highlight of a visit to the waterfront is the **Two Oceans Aquarium** (open daily 9.30am–6pm; admission fee; tel: 021-418 3823, <www.aquarium.co.za>), which brims with marine life of all shapes and dimensions, from seahorses and

The life aquatic at Cape Town's Two Oceans Aquarium

sea urchins to great white sharks and Cape fur seals. A rocky walk-in aviary is inhabited by black oystercatchers, African penguins, and rockhopper penguins – the latter distinguished by its foppish yellow eyebrows.

Table Mountain

People have been climbing **Table Mountain** at least since 1503, when the Portuguese mariner Antonio de Saldanha went up to check the lie of the land and sea. Today, climbers can choose from 350 routes to the 1,087-m (3,565-ft) summit of the shale, sandstone and granite flattop. The climb can be dangerous, however, so amateurs are warned to start early, be certain of the weather and dress suitably (wear sensible shoes and carry some warm clothing, just in case). Guides are available to show you the way.

Alternatively, you can take the easy way – in seven minutes. The cable car has been whisking passengers to the top, and down again, since 1929. There's plenty of room on top to roam, with maps and telescopes there. If the weather starts to deteriorate, a siren recalls visitors to the cable car station for a return to earth before service is suspended. In good weather, the cars operate half hourly from May to November from 8.30am to 6pm; from December to April from 8am to 10pm (tel: 021-424 8181). If you're using public transport, take the city bus for 'Kloof Nek' from Adderley Street. A bus run by the Cableway Company takes you on to the lower cable terminus.

For a spectacular picture of Table Mountain you may want to sign up for an aerial tour of the peninsula. Check with the tourist office, Captour (tel: 021-405 4500). On land, northwards around Table Bay on the M14 highway, the road closes in on the sand dunes for a head-on view of the mighty cliff, with silhouettes of Devil's Peak and Lion's Head.

THE CAPE PENINSULA

The Cape of Good Hope is as gripping a part of the world as you'll ever see and the sights on the way are worth stopping for. There are two likely routes for exploring around the 50-km (31-mile) long peninsula. The more leisurely one starts out along the coast, counterclockwise from central Cape Town and the waterfront, passing South Africa's oldest working lighthouse at **Green Point**. Ferries make the 11½-km (7-mile) trip out to **Robben Island**, interesting for its flora and African (or jackass) penguins, but famous for Nelson Mandela's imprisonment here. Groups are limited, so bookings must be made in advance (tel: 021-413 4200).

Sea Point is an in-town beach resort with a fashionable promenade and high-rent, high-rise buildings of all kinds of architectural style. For miles beyond, the road reveals beach after beach alternating with rocky coves. Clifton Bay, with four beaches, is the most popular. The season is at its height from mid-October to mid-March. Along the Atlantic Coast, however, the water is cold all year round. For tolerable sea temperatures, visit the opposite shore of the peninsula and the warmer waters of False Bay.

A penguin on Robben Island

The road soon turns inland along the slopes of the **Twelve Apostles** mountain formation (actually a continuation of the back of Table Mountain). The highway returns to sea level at the big semi-circular fishing harbour of **Hout Bay**. Although some yachts are moored here, Hout Bay is obviously a working port. At certain times of the

Chapman's Peak Drive

year the industrial aspects overwhelm the scenery, when factories producing fish meal and fish oil emit their vapours. Hout Bay is also an important source of a tasty South African delicacy, smoked *snoek* and there are some good seafood restaurants.

A favourite excursion from here is by launch to some rocks known as **Duiker Island**, out beyond the calm of the harbour. Hundreds of seals can be seen diving and playing, the youngsters being cajoled into the sea to learn how to cope, the old-timers lolling on the rocks. Cormorants, gulls and oystercatchers perch wing to wing on available spaces.

Past Hout Bay, the Marine Drive rises to its climax – a corniche that hangs between cliffs and sea. When **Chapman's Peak Drive** was undertaken during World War I, it was considered to be a breakthrough in road engineering. There is a lookout point at the highest spot on the drive, which re-opened in 2004, after several years of maintenance work. The route soon swerves inland and crosses the Cape Peninsula, now hardly 10km (6 miles) wide. At the eastern extremity lies the small town of **Fish Hoek**, a good spot for swimming.

The other way from Cape Town to Fish Hoek is by the inland route. The M3 highway exits town as a busy but well-landscaped boulevard, passing the Groote Schuur Hospital, where, in 1967, Professor Christiaan Barnard led the team that performed the first transplant of a human heart.

On the slopes of Devil's Peak, the **Rhodes Memorial** is an impressive monument to the financier/statesman. In a simulated Greek Temple at the top of cascading granite steps, a bust of Cecil Rhodes looks out over what was his favourite panorama.

The oldest university in South Africa is set in priceless forested surroundings beneath Devil's Peak. The University of Cape Town, founded in 1829, has both traditional, ivy-covered buildings and stark modern ones, including the Baxter Theatre, an intellectual focus for the city as well as for the university.

About 3km (2 miles) past the UCT campus it's a short side trip off the M3 to **Kirstenbosch** (open daily Apr–Aug 8am–6pm; Sept–Mar 8am–7pm; admission fee; tel: 021-799 8783), a renowned botanical garden. Thousands of plant species grow here – representing nearly a quarter of all the types found in South Africa. (Because of the country's varied climates no single botanical garden can cover the entire range.) From August to early October is the most exciting time to visit.

Cape Dutch

Dramatic landscapes add to the visual impact of the Cape's old country seats – large white houses, often with thatched roofs. Cape Dutch architecture features symmetrical gables with curves and baroque intricacies, window shutters, wide main doors with fanlights and airy interiors with timbered ceilings.

One of the most magnificent Cape Dutch houses – **Groot Constantia**, south of Kirstenbosch – is now a museum. Since the turn of the 18th century, this farm has been producing great wines. Part of the old cellars, behind the main house, has been turned into a wine museum. The main museum, which occupies the homestead itself, includes antique furniture, porcelain, implements and glassware.

False Bay

To make the most of a tour round the peninsula's coast, set out early, as the sun rises above the Hottentots-Holland Mountains and shimmers on the surface of **False Bay**. About 30km (19 miles) wide, the bay has a number of tantalising beaches.

An elegant Cape Dutch mansion

Situated 20km (12 miles) from the centre of Cape Town, on the east coast, is the booming resort of **Muizenberg**, with endless dunes of almost snow-white sand. The sea here is good for swimming between November and April.

The suburban railway from Cape Town will take you to **Simonstown**, the main base of the South African navy. You can spot frigates and mine sweepers here and many a desirable yacht. An unusual monument to Simonstown's past as a British naval base is the **Martello Tower**, somewhat hidden from view inside the dockyard area. This cylindrical stone fort, built in 1796, is thought to be the oldest of its kind in the world. Now restored, it serves as a museum of naval mementoes.

Even though lighthouses, paved roads and a restaurant have been added, the **Cape of Good Hope Nature Reserve**, part of the recently gazetted **Cape Peninsula National Park**, remains virtually intact in its primeval state. Driving along the lesser roads you might come across the rare bontebok, as well as eland, springbok, ostrich and other wildlife. Baboons, unfortunately, are legion. Signs warn visitors not to feed them (and if you leave your car, lock it up with the windows closed as baboons loot from unsecured vehicles). Specialists are fascinated by the flora – mostly low shrubs and grass. Everyone enjoys the outbursts of colour from wild protea and heather.

The reserve's long coastline varies from cliffs to rocky flats and sandy coves, but the high spot is where the roads run out, at **Cape Point**. A small tram called the Flying Dutchman shuttles visitors from the car park (parking lot) to the top of the final hill. From there you can walk to various observation points, the highest at the base of the original 1860 lighthouse. The new 19 million-candle lighthouse is purportedly the most powerful in the world.

At Cape Point, the granite cliffs plunge 259m (850ft) to the sea – South Africa's tallest sea cliffs. Giant rollers boil and froth at the base, while cormorants fight the shrieking wind to reach their ledges. Albatross, gannets, gulls and giant petrels share the fishing in this tormented sea.

Searching for the route to India, the Portuguese explorer Bartolomeu Dias rounded the Cape for the first time in 1488. Unable to see it due to a raging storm, he wrote on his map, 'Cape of Storms'. Although it was later renamed the Cape of Good Hope, Dias was lost at sea in the same waters 12 years later.

Looking west, you see the Cape of Good Hope itself, not Africa's southernmost tip, which is actually Cape Agulhas near Bredasdorp, but still spectacular. The spot is accessible from the road, so you can climb the rocks near sea level for a closer look at the breaking waves.

Simonsberg Mountain overlooks the vineyards around Stellenbosch

WINE COUNTRY

South African wines originate in a small corner of the country within a 162-km (100-mile) radius of Cape Town. The soils and microclimates within this arc are so varied that all manner of wines can be produced, from sweet and dry whites to rosés, reds and fortified types in the style of sherry and port.

One-day excursions offered by tour operators cover two principal centres, Stellenbosch and Paarl. You could do the trip yourself and take in some other stops as well. The tourist information offices of both regions issue maps and brochures and can suggest itineraries. The scenery itself is enchanting.

Stellenbosch

Less than 50km (31 miles) east of central Cape Town, **Stellenbosch** has a wealth of beautiful old buildings. It's an endearing, relaxed university town named after the great 17th-century wine enthusiast, Governor Van der Stel. Fires destroyed the original thatched cottages and the best of the buildings on view today date from between 1775 and 1820.

Grosvenor House, an early 19th-century mansion with an award-winning garden, is filled with Old Cape furnishings. **Schreuder House** (1709), with simple settlers' furnishings, is possibly the country's oldest surviving town house. A homestead of 1780 houses the **Rembrandt Van Rijn Art Gallery**. In the same compound a wine museum displays old Roman amphoras and antique glasses and bottles. Nearby is a museum featuring the history and technology of brandy-making.

Around Stellenbosch, vineyards spread for miles over hillsides and valleys, against a backdrop of imposing mountains. About 50 **wine estates** and cooperatives in the district welcome visitors daily (some close on Saturday afternoon and Sunday), usually offering scheduled cellar tours, wine tastings and opportunities to buy. Look out for the 'Wine Route' logo.

On Stellenbosch's outskirts, **Rustenberg Wine Estate** (tel: 021-809 1200), with its orchards and gabled dairy, is one of the most beautiful in the Cape. As is **Vergelegen** (tel: 021-847 1334, <www.vergelegen.co.za>), whose name means 'Far Away', referring to its location on the once remote

Cape Wine

Stellenbosch and Paarl, the main and probably most versatile of the Cape wine regions, offer the best of everything: rich reds, crisp whites, ports in true Portuguese style, Sauterne-like sweet Noble Late Harvest wines and some excellent value-for-money Cap Classiques.

Franschhoek, a valley of boutique wineries, offers mostly white wines, with a handful of red gems. Then there's Constantia, with a select range of classical whites and reds nurtured in historic Cape Dutch cellars. Walker Bay is the place for some of the Cape's benchmark Pinot Noirs and Chardonnays, and a taste of pioneering Pinotages.

footslopes of the Helderberg Mountains south of Stellenbosch. Founded in 1700, the manor house, decorated in period style, is a fine example of Cape Dutch architecture.

To the southwest, **Franschhoek** (literally French Corner) is named after the Huguenots, who settled there in the 18th century. Framed by lofty blue peaks, Franschhoek is ideal for an al fresco lunch, either in town, at one of eight highly-rated restaurants, or at the historic

Franschhoek vineyard

Boschendal Estate (tel: 021-870 4200, <www.boschendal. com>), where you can have a picnic before visiting the cellars.

Paarl

The Cape's other main wine region centres on the 18th-century town of **Paarl**, about 60km (37 miles) from Cape Town, just off the N1 motorway. It's about twice the size of Stellenbosch, with a huge modern civic centre that also houses the information office. The long main street is lined with historic buildings, working vineyards and the headquarters of KWV, the Cooperative Wine Growers Association. Tours are scheduled four times a day. The **Old Parsonage (Oude Pastorie) Museum**, in a perfectly restored, 18th-century Cape Dutch building, has a fine collection of old Cape furniture and silver.

Elsewhere in Paarl and the surrounding Berg River Valley are numerous **wine estates** and cooperative cellars. Most have wines for sale, with or without tastings, and cellar tours either on a schedule or by arrangement.

The more time you have, the more treasures you will be able to discover in this part of the Cape. **Ceres**, a pretty town at the heart of a rich fruit-growing region, is well worth a visit; and **Tulbagh**, which dates from the early 18th century, has some of the most beautiful Cape Dutch houses of all.

CAPE TOWN TO JOHANNESBURG

You can fly back to Johannesburg, of course, but if you have time you'll see more of the country by driving or taking the train, either the regular service or the luxury Blue Train.

The railway and the direct road both cross **Great Karoo**, a vast semi-desert. Despite a lack of rainfall, some fascinating forms of plant life are able to flourish here and in places water is pumped up from bore holes to sustain the flocks of sheep. If you're travelling by car, **Kimberley** is a convenient overnight stop. The former mining town's famous **Big Hole** is about 1.5km (1 mile) round and half as deep, the excavation at the

---

The Blue Train

The 1,608-km (997-mile), 26-hour journey on the Blue Train between Cape Town and Pretoria via Johannesburg is one of the world's most luxurious. A five-star hotel on wheels, it offers three-room suites – lounge, bedroom and bathroom – or simpler quarters. The designers thought of everything: a thin layer of gold on the double windows reduces heat and glare; venetian blinds between the panes operate electrically; and air springs guarantee a quiet, smooth ride.

After a champagne farewell, the 16-car train sets off. Lounge in the bar, dine handsomely (the price includes meals) and gaze outside as Table Mountain and the Cape vineyards gradually give way to the semi-desert of the Great Karoo. The approach to Johannesburg is indicated by the truncated pyramids of gold-mine waste heaps. For reservations tel: 012-334 8459; fax: 012-334 8464; <www.bluetrain.co.za>.

The Blue Train offers a highly luxurious way to view South Africa

top of this 'pipe' from the earth's depths was the source of over 14 million carats of diamonds between 1871 and 1914.

It looks far on the map, but good roads and light traffic mean that the journey from the Cape to Jo'burg is an easy two-day trip. An alternative to the shortest route involves only a few hours' more driving. Head north up the Western Cape through lovely scenery (and in September, spectacular wild flowers) to **Springbok**, then east via **Upington**. It's a short diversion to the **Augrabies Falls**, where the Orange River thunders over the escarpment, forming one of the world's great waterfalls.

Having come so far, adventurous sorts will be tempted to see South Africa's strangest extremity, its piece of the Kalahari Desert. A tongue of territory jutting out between Namibia and Botswana, the **Kgalagadi Transfrontier Park** is reached by ◀ dusty but well-graded roads. The park has excellent accommodation and other facilities. While here, you may catch sight of gemsbok, springbok, lions and, if you're lucky, cheetahs, too.

WHAT TO DO

SPORTS

South Africans are dedicated to the outdoor life. Half the country seems to be wielding fishing rods or golf clubs, running, swimming or riding surfboards. The other half is likely to be watching cricket, rugby, football, wrestling or racing. In general, sporting stars tend to receive more publicity and acclaim than film celebrities or politicians. South African Tourism *(see page 123)* and CATASA (Council of Adventure Travel Agents of Southern Africa, tel: 014-189 2417) can provide useful details about sporting activities and tour operations.

Watersports

South Africa's 2,800km (1,740 miles) of coastline caters for all tastes. In parts of KwaZulu-Natal and the Eastern and Western Cape, dunes stretch endlessly into total wilderness. If you prefer convenience and crowds, the popular resorts have all the facilities. Because of sharks and tricky tides, swim only where signs indicate it's safe. The busier beaches have lifeguards on duty. If the waves are too high or the sea is uncomfortably cold (as the Atlantic often is), you can fall back on the hotel swimming pool.

Surfing has become a South African passion. The waves of the Eastern Cape are fit for champions, with often impeccable conditions to be found at Cape St Francis and Jeffrey's Bay, and warmer waters in the Durban area. For information, contact the United Surfing Council of South Africa: <www.surfingsouthafrica.co.za>.

Windsurfing (boardsailing) is the fastest-growing water sport in South Africa, from the Indian Ocean to the chilly

Hot-air ballooning in the Magaliesberg Mountains *(see page 87)*

Atlantic (where wetsuits are standard) and on lakes inland. Check with the South African Windsurfing Class Association (tel: 011-726 7076) for those areas that require permits for offshore windsurfing. Old-fashioned sailing hasn't lost its allure, with dozens of yacht clubs offering facilities and classes at all levels.

For still more varied thrills, **white-water rafting** trips are offered on the stretch of the Orange River near Augrabies Falls; contact the Kalahari Adventure Centre (tel: 054-451 0177, <www.kalahari.co.za>) for details. You'll find **scuba diving** schools and clubs in the vicinity of all the main coastal resorts. Contact the South African Underwater Union (tel: 021-930 6549).

Trout fishing

Fishing

Whether they prefer rock, surf, or deep-sea fishing, anglers will have a field day in South Africa. Everything they could dream of can be found in the South Atlantic and Indian oceans. The oceans' meeting point, near Cape Town, is said to be the home of more kinds of game fish than any other sea; for instance, in the past all species of marlin and tunny (tuna) have been landed here. In the big ports, such as Cape Town and Durban, you can take part in organised **deep-sea excursions**. Elsewhere, small, powerful ski boats may be hired to reach the action.

The best seasons for rock and surf fishing vary with the region. In the Western Cape, it's from January to April, but along the Kwa-Zulu-Natal coast the most promising time is from June to November. There is un-paralleled excitement in June between Port St Johns

> **Inland, rivers and lakes all over the country offer the chance to fish for trout, bass, and carp. There are strict catch limits in most places and permits are required; contact the local parks board or Department of Nature Conservation for permit and catch requirements.**

and Durban: immense shoals of sardines run along the coast, attracting shark, barracuda, kingfish and shad, which in turn lure anglers to the scene. If you want to join the cray-fish (rock lobster) hunt, you will need a licence, and there are seasonal restrictions for these and for oysters and abalone (here called *perlemoen*).

Participation Sports

Saturday is the most important day of the week for organised sports in South Africa. While for many years sporting activities of any importance were banned on Sundays, games are played regularly on this day, too.

Golf has been played in South Africa for well over a cen-tury and there are several courses of international repute. Many courses welcome visitors, at least on weekdays, when even the public courses are not normally overcrowded. It's worth contacting club secretaries for starting times and to check dress codes. The South African Golf Association can also advise: <www.saga.co.za>. Golf is played all the year round, but over most of the country the greens are at their best from December to March. Carry an umbrella for those inevitable afternoon rainstorms.

The good weather makes year-round **tennis** a possibility, too. The equivalent of Wimbledon in South Africa, Ellis Park in Johannesburg has 21 tennis courts. The Wanderers is one of more than 170 tennis clubs in the city and has 26 courts. Most of the resort hotels either have their own courts or else have access to facilities nearby; for more information call the South African Tennis Association (tel: 011-442 0500, <www.satennis.co.za>). In addition, some of the hotels also have **squash** courts.

The tranquil-looking, but nevertheless highly competitive, British game of **bowls** arrived early in South Africa, spreading from Port Elizabeth to KwaZulu-Natal and the Rand. Today 60,000 bowlers belong to some 800 clubs; visiting players from abroad are welcomed.

A growing interest in the **martial arts** has an obvious link with self-defence in the city streets. **Mountain biking** has be-

Horse riding on the Eastern Cape

come as much a passion with the young as it has in many Western countries, but a game called **jukskei** seems to be home-grown: in the same way that Americans throw horse shoes, Afrikaners have taken to throwing sticks.

South Africa's varied and often dramatic landscape offers plenty of opportunities for unusual and extreme activities. You could try sandboarding down huge coastal dunes (tel: 021-422 0388, <www.downhilladventures.com>) or bungee jumping from Bloukrans Bridge, the highest in Africa (tel: 042-281 1458, <www.faceadrenalin.com>.

Outdoor Activities

Horse riding and associated sports take place across the republic. The Johannesburg area alone has 20 riding schools, and out in the wilds some country hotels have their own stables. Pony treks are arranged by KZN Wildlife (tel: 033-845 1000/1999, <www.kznwildlife.com>) in the Drakensberg Mountains.

A series of **hiking** trails is being developed which will eventually reach from the mountains of the Cape to the northern Transvaal. A booklet with all hiking trail booking details is available from the Hiking Federation of South Africa (tel: 012-327 0083, <www.hiking-south-africa.info>).

It's quite costly, but you can go **hot-air ballooning** in the Magaliesberg Mountains near Johannesburg or in the Drakensberg Mountains, KwaZulu-Natal, where you'll also see hang gliders doing their stuff. In fact, if any form of sport or exercise catches on anywhere in the world, you can be sure that it will soon find popularity in South Africa.

The successful conservation of the game herds means that for some species there has to be a culling programme, and this opens up the possibility of **hunting**. Details of quotas and costs and other information can be obtained from South African Tourism (*see pages 123–4*).

Spectator Sports

Horse racing takes place year-round at tracks in all the major cities. The race of the year is the Durban July Handicap, which is run on the first Saturday of July. The Metropolitan Stakes, held at Kenilworth Race Course in Cape Town, is an important social event usually held in January.

The **motor racing** circuit at Kyalami, north of Johannesburg, hosts a range of motor and motorbike racing events throughout the year.

Rugby, **cricket** and **football** have practically attained religious status among participants and spectators alike. Although efforts are being made to provide black South Africans with better playing facilities, rugby is still a predominantly white pursuit. You can see top-class matches at the huge Ellis Park stadium in Johannesburg, at Newlands in Cape Town, and indeed in every city and town throughout the winter. Other popular spectator sports include boxing, wrestling and athletics.

A National Passion

Today sport in South Africa is able to transcend race and politics. Once it laid the lines of segregation bare. For years, only the largely white sports – rugby, cricket, golf – received necessary funds for development.

Great strides have been made since South Africa's readmission to the international arena. In a spirit of reconciliation, Nelson Mandela donned a Springbok jersey following their victory in the 1995 rugby World Cup final. Soccer is big among blacks, and the national team defied the odds to lift the African Nations Cup trophy in 1996, reaching the World Cup finals in 1998 and 2002. All South African sporting bodies have tried to create a more equal sporting society. The United Cricket Board set up an impressive development programme in the townships and rural areas. Another great boost – South Africa will host the 2010 football World Cup.

SHOPPING

South Africa's shops are remarkably diverse – from flea markets and quaint bazaars to air-conditioned boutiques and big-city shopping malls vast enough for hours of browsing.

Visitors buying more expensive items, or a lot of cheaper ones, can reclaim the value-added tax (VAT) at their point of departure from the country. To do so they must show the items concerned as well as proper VAT receipts.

With its rich mix of cultures, South Africa has an abundance of artists and craftsmen, including painters and sculptors, glass-blowers, jewellery-makers, furniture-

Vibrant fabrics on sale in Greenmarket Square, Cape Town

makers, and weavers and spinners, who produce hand-knitted garments and painted fabrics. Arts and crafts routes enable visitors to see the artists and view their work in their studios. Ask the local tourist association for details and maps regarding arts and crafts routes and markets in the area you're visiting.

When considering a purchase of arts or crafts, ask about the item's provenance. Old (antique) South African beadwork and San (Bushman) curios are very rare.

What to Buy
African curios. There's no end to the supply of tribal shields, spears and masks, most of which are produced by the manual

> Most countries now ban imports of ivory in order to prevent the poaching of elephants. This ban also applies to elephant tusks that result from the legitimate, controlled hunting of elephants in Kruger National Park.

equivalent of assembly lines. Some of the more artistic designs and older items come from other countries, in particular the Democratic Republic of Congo, Ghana and Côte d'Ivoire.

Beads. Early traders from Europe brought glass beads to exchange for ivory or other valuable commodities. Now European tourists buy beadwork necklaces and ornaments in various bright geometric designs.

Chess sets. Figurines of African warriors represent the pawns, medicine men the bishops, and so on.

Diamonds. Jewellers licensed by the South African customs give duty-free preference to bona-fide foreign visitors on diamonds that are cut, ground and polished but not set. Semi-precious stones, which also abound here, come closer to most budgets: these include agate, amethyst, jasper, rose quartz and verdite.

Indian spices. Curry powders and chilli peppers with explosive colours and flavours are fitting souvenirs of Durban.

Jewellery. Certain jewellers with special customs licences are able to sell gold pendants, chains and earrings to visitors without charging the stiff levels of South African duty. You will have to show your passport, air ticket and flight reservation to qualify.

Krugerrands. Collectors of gold will always be pleased to receive one, or a set, of these desirable and portable South African coins. They may be purchased duty-free for foreign currency in the departure lounge of Johannesburg's Jan Smuts Airport.

Musical instruments. You will soon learn to play one of those small bush xylophones with metal spikes and a carved wooden base. You can also take home a small drum-rattle or a big carved drum to thump.

Pottery. African artisans produce coiled pots with ancient tribal designs or thrown pots with original motifs.

Rugs and tapestries. Handwoven in geometric or figurative designs, these are suitable for wall-hangings or carpets. From spinning wheel to final trimming, some of these works of rural art are produced with meticulous care.

Seashells and coral. Those vast beaches turn up seashells which serious collectors covet. Coral fantasies, although controversial, are sold in curio shops on the coast and inland.

Straw goods. Bags, baskets, hats, mats and trays are often sold in souvenir shops or by the roadside at makeshift stalls.

Straw goods are a mainstay of South African crafts

Wines. Quality wines and local versions of sherries, ports and brandies make natural souvenirs of the Cape (*see pages 78 and 99–100*).

Woodcraft. Salad bowls, meat trays, spoons and ladles are readily available. Wooden sculptures run from miniature rhinos to large, elaborate carvings incorporating entire tribes of figures. The fine-grained local hardwoods make solid furniture and fine carvings. Don't be put off by the name given to stinkwood – it only smells when freshly cut.

Grahamstown Festival sax

ENTERTAINMENT

The big cities, townships, and resort towns have **nightclubs** and a lively nightlife, mostly in or near the major hotels. In Johannesburg, the Melville area is now the most popular place to go for live music, restaurants, and clubs. When you go out at night, avoid wearing conspicuous jewellery and carrying large amounts of cash. For details of the latest venues, live music performances, and other current events, consult the local press or tourist board publications such as *Hello Johannesburg*, *Hello Cape Town,* or the weekly *Mail & Guardian* newspaper.

Regulations governing alcohol are not as strict as they used to be. Shops are forbidden from selling it on Sundays, but it is served at all licensed restaurants and bars.

In the major cities, lively professional **theatres** present plays in either English or Afrikaans. Some of the most important include the State Theatre in Pretoria, Johannesburg's Civic Theatre and Cape Town's Baxter Theatre. The National Symphony Orchestra performs in the major centres and there are a number of accomplished opera and ballet companies.

Cinemas show current international film releases, and the high level of censorship associated with the apartheid era has been greatly relaxed. There are several performances daily and advance booking is available.

In larger towns and cities, tickets to films, plays and concerts may be bought at *Computicket* stores, a computerised booking agency (tel: 011-340 8000, <www.computicket.com>). Consult the local papers for current information on performances.

Calendar of Events

January *Cape Minstrels Carnival*, Cape Town.

February *Dias Festival*, Mossel Bay, Western Cape.

March *Cape Town International Jazz Festival*.

March–April *Klein Karoo National Arts Festival*, Oudtshoorn – week-long festival featuring pop and rock acts, classical music, drama and dance. *Rand Show* (two weeks around Easter), Johannesburg – the largest trade exposition in South Africa. *Jeffrey's Bay Shell Festival*, Eastern Cape.

April *Port Elizabeth Splash Festival*, Hobie Beach, Port Elizabeth. *Music in the Mountains Festival*, Drakensberg Boys School, KwaZulu-Natal. *Old Mutual Two Oceans Marathon*, Cape Town. *Tulbagh Goes Dutch Festival* – celebrations of the town's Cape Dutch heritage.

May *Cape Gourmet Festival*, Cape Town – two-week event held at venues across the city. *Rooms on View International Decor Fair*, Sandton, Gauteng.

June *Comrades Marathon*, KwaZulu-Natal – gruelling international marathon alternately run between Durban and Pietermaritzburg. *Durban International Film Festival*, University of Natal, Durban.

June–July *National Arts Festival*, Grahamstown, Eastern Cape – a fortnight of drama, dance, visual arts, music and film.

July *Knysna Oyster Festival*, Knysna, Western Cape. *Biltong Festival*, Somerset East, Eastern Cape – Afrikaner country festival. *Bushveld Festival*, Ellisras, Limpopo Province. *Hibiscus Festival*, South Coast, KwaZulu-Natal.

August *Hermanus Wine and Food Fair*, Western Cape.

August–September *Pretoria Show* – long running agricultural show.

September *Arts Alive*, various venues, Johannesburg – month-long celebration of the performing arts. *North-West Cultural Calabash*, Taung – recommended African arts festival. *Whale Festival*, Hermanus, Western Cape. *Zulu King's Reed Dance*, eNyokeni Palace, Eshowe, KwaZulu-Natal.

September–October *Magoebaskloof Spring Festival*, Limpopo Province.

October *Food and Wine Festival*, Stellenbosch, Western Cape. *Jacaranda Festival*, Market Square, Pretoria.

November *Cherry Festival*, Ficksburg, Free State.

December *Rustler's Valley New Year Celebration*, Ficksburg, Free State.

EATING OUT

With 13 million head of cattle on South African ranchland and two oceans to provide the fish, you're assured of good food in abundance. Cooking here has the old-fashioned virtues – it's wholesome and there's plenty of it. You may indeed be daunted by the sizes of the portions. In many restaurants 'doggy bags' are called for, in the American way, so that the excess can be taken home

City restaurants come in all varieties, from five-star haute cuisine and elegance down to the most utilitarian fast-food joint. Italian, French, Chinese and Portuguese/Mozambican cuisines abound, but Johannesburg claims ethnic restaurants of 20 nationalities, including Japanese, Korean, Greek, Indonesian, Turkish and Mexican. Many Cape restaurants serve old Cape Dutch and Malay recipes. Durban is noted for its Indian restaurants, and offers the cuisines of various regions of that continent.

> You might wish to consider timing your visit to South Africa to coincide with a food festival, such as the South African Cheese Festival held at Paarl from late April to early May, <www.cheesefestival.co.za>, the Gourmet Festival held at Cape Town in late May, <www.gourmetsa.com>, or early July's Knysna Oyster Festival, <www.oysterfestival.co.za>.

In South Africa, the term café is conventionally applied to a small store similar in nature to the British corner shop. Cafés of this sort often serve cheap greasy take-away food and soft drinks, but will have nowhere to sit down and eat. In cities, however, the more familiar sit-down café has become an increasingly commonplace feature of post-apartheid South Africa, in particular the popular News Café chain.

In all hotels except, paradoxically, the most expensive, breakfast will normally be included in the price. Even if it isn't, it's likely to be good value, typically consisting of fresh fruit and juice, hot or cold cereals, bacon or sausage, eggs, toast and rolls, butter and marmalade and tea or coffee. Many hotels have breakfast buffets in the Scandinavian manner, though the dishes on offer are more British in derivation, as is the morning 'wake-up' coffee or tea that you can have brought to your room.

At the game lodges it makes sense to take that coffee or tea at dawn or before, then go out looking for the wildlife prior to returning for a hearty mid-morning breakfast or brunch.

Fish and Seafood

All along the coast you'll find fish restaurants that clearly have good connections down at the harbour. But the majority

Fishermen unloading the catch of the day in Durban

of restaurants, specialist or not, have fish on the menu – and usually fresh. Cape salmon is a tasty white fish, unrelated to the salmon of Europe and North America. *Kabeljou* is similar to cod. *Kingklip*, a large meaty fish, makes fine fillets. *Snoek,* a cold-water fish about a yard long, is served smoked as a starter or grilled as a main course, while *Steenbras* resembles sea bream.

The excellent shellfish is worth seeking out: mussels, *perlemoen* (abalone), prawns (the latter often imported from Mozambique). The local crayfish (elsewhere called spiny rock lobster) is a delicacy. Oysters may be served with hot sauce already applied – remember to specify in advance if you want yours unadulterated.

Meat

South Africa's favourite food is *braaivleis* (barbecued meat), a feast cooked in the garden or at a picnic spot. Men are generally in charge and the whole business is taken seriously: special cuts of meat are sold for the purpose, and hardwood is selected for its proper fire-making qualities.

Braai

If you can eat it, you can *braai* it. Originally an Afrikaner social tradition, the barbecueing of large quantities of meat and any other food to hand is something of a national institution in South Africa. Each weekend, wood fires are lit in countless gardens for the family *braaivleis* (in Afrikaans *braai* means to grill, *vleis* means meat).

The most popular foods to barbecue are lamb chops, curried *sosaties* (skewered meat), *boerewors* (spicy beef or pork sausages), *biltong* (dry, salted meat) and freshly picked corn on the cob. The secret of a good *braai* is to cook the meat as slowly as possible while keeping it moist with marinade.

The *braaivleis* is part of the South African way of life

You may be invited to a *braai (see box opposite)* or you can buy the meats and the wood and use the barbecue you'll find outside most chalets or rondavels in game park camps. Otherwise, the many steak houses serve a pretty good approximation of the outdoor taste. The steaks – fillet, rump, sirloin, tournedos, or T-bone – are invariably big, thick and tender. Whether you ask for it or not, the cook is liable to grill them with a barbecue sauce. A number of other sauces are usually on the menu, the most piquant being 'monkey gland' sauce (hot sauce and chutney).

In steak houses and other restaurants you'll also find a variety of alternatives: lamb, veal, pork, poultry and game. All dishes come with potatoes (usually chips – French fries – or baked) or, less commonly, rice and cooked vegetables – beans, broccoli, carrots, mushrooms, pumpkin, squash, sweet potatoes or *mealies* (corn on the cob). Steak houses and some other restaurants may have salad bars in the

American style – a big choice of nutritious raw vegetables and dressings to mix and match.

Local Favourites

Don't miss the traditional South African meat dishes, particularly *bobotie*, a baked minced-meat recipe from the Cape. It's probably of Malay origin, with its additions of apricot, almond, chutney, and a subtle spicing of curry. *Boerewors* is a flavourful country sausage, usually of a beef and pork combination. *Bredie* is a rich ragout, usually of mutton, with a thick tomato sauce. *Sosaties* are kebabs, resembling Southeast Asia's *satés*, little pieces of lamb marinated in vinegar, sugar, garlic, curry powder and apricot. Varieties of smoked pork are another local speciality.

Enjoying a meal in Cape Town

Biltong, strips of dried meat, was once made out of necessity, to take on treks and for preserving surplus meat before the days of refrigeration. Now it's something of a delicacy. *Biltong* is most often made with beef, but game *biltong* – from various antelopes and ostrich – is also widely available.

Desserts

If you have space, there may be apple pie, *melktert* (minimal pastry and a light, gently spiced custard), cheesecake, or trifle in the English style (sponge cake smothered in fruit, nuts, custard and whipped cream). Then, of course, there's always fresh fruit – small, sweet pineapples, bananas of various kinds, melons, apples, grapes and *naartjies* (mandarin oranges). Also, look out for homemade ice-cream with real fruit flavours.

> The arrival of the Huguenots in 1688 brought a French influence to South African cuisine. Settling in the Franschhoek valley, they harvested fruit and produced wine. The Afrikaans term for fruit preserves and jams, *konfyt*, comes from the French technique for preserving food by long, slow simmering – *confit*.

Excellent South African versions of many European cheeses – including brie, camembert, cheddar, gouda, mozzarella and so on – are hardly distinguishable from the originals, except that their price is lower.

Before you've finished your dessert the waiter may present you with the bill. This is not intended to hurry you out. Nevertheless, it is rare for South Africans to linger at the table after a meal.

Wine and Other Drinks

Cape wines have come a long way. The early settlers grew the classic grape varieties, but the same plague that ravaged the vines in Europe in the 1880s also struck South Africa, and the country's vineyards had to be replanted with resistant American grafts.

Today, the most widely planted white grape is Chenin Blanc, sometimes known locally as Steen, and used to make anything from bone dry whites to brandy. Other popular white varieties include Chardonnay, Sauvignon Blanc and Colombar (the latter used mostly for dessert and brandy). Common red varieties include Cabernet Sauvignon, Merlot, Syrah (normally referred to as Shiraz in South Africa) and Pinotage, a cross between Pinot Noir and Cinsaut (Hermitage) pioneered in the Cape in the 1920s *(see also the box on page 78)*.

Aside from wine, there are lager-style beers (served very cold), well-known brands of soft drinks (called cool drinks) and mineral waters. Fruit juices, freshly squeezed or pasteurised, are delicious. Look out for some of the exotic mixtures: guava, lime, mango, apricot, peach and pear. You won't cause any surprise by asking for tap water, which is drinkable everywhere.

Bear in mind that some restaurants lack wine or liquor licences, especially in Cape Town, so it is wise to check in advance. South Africans often bring their own wine to licence-less restaurants If you don't, it's no good expecting to go to a nearby wine shop: they open only during normal shopping hours and never on Sunday.

The Cape is renowned for its viniculture

HANDY TRAVEL TIPS

An A–Z Summary of Practical Information

A

ACCOMMODATION (see also CAMPING AND CARAVANNING, YOUTH AND BACKPACKER HOSTELS and RECOMMENDED HOTELS)

The South African Tourism board publishes a directory of hotels with ratings – five stars for the pinnacle of luxury, one star for simple comforts. At the top level you can expect a swimming pool, tennis courts, sauna, choice of restaurants and bars and air-conditioning throughout. The prices match the standards, but the degree of comfort of hotels at the lower end of the scale is also notable. Many two-star establishments, for instance, have spacious air-conditioned rooms, and one-star hotels have a high percentage of rooms with private baths.

The directory also includes luxury lodges and rest camps in game parks, beach cottages, holiday flats, and caravan and campsites, and can be obtained, or ordered, from South African Tourism's national and international offices *(see pages 123–4)*; it is invaluable for planning ahead, for use on arrival, and while you're touring. In resort areas, mid-range and family-orientated accommodation catering mostly or partially to the local leisure market is normally heavily booked over South African school holiday periods (December to January, Easter, June to July and early October). By contrast, city hotels catering mostly to the local business market are typically busy on Monday to Thursday nights and are quieter over the weekend, when discounted rates may be available. Upmarket accommodation and backpacker hostels servicing the international market tend to be busiest during the main inbound tourist season, which generally runs from September to May. At other times, reduced off-season prices may apply.

Among many other details, the directory reports the status of every establishment's alcohol licence (if any), its policy on pets, whether there is wheelchair access, and gives an indication of price which, because of inflation, may be outdated. Prices include VAT at the standard rate.

AIRPORTS

South Africa's principal airport, Johannesburg International Airport, is about 24km (15 miles) from Johannesburg and 60km (37 miles) from Pretoria. Services in the terminal include restaurants and bars, shops, hairdresser, pharmacy, florist, post office, bank, insurance and car-hire (rental) desks and duty-free shops. For airport enquiries, tel: 011-921 6262.

Metered taxis are available. An airport bus runs to and from the South African Airways (SAA; tel: 0861-359 722 or 011-978 5313, <www.flysaa.com>) terminal (called the Rotunda) opposite Johannesburg's main railway station, leaving every 30 minutes from 5am to 10pm. The trip takes about half an hour. For enquiries to the SAA terminal, tel: 0861-606 606 or 011-978 1000.

Another bus service links the airport and Sandton City, and there is also a service to and from Pretoria (leaving the city SAA terminal).

Other international airports are at Durban and Cape Town. Durban Airport is 16km (10 miles) southwest of the city, and is served by a bus service to the SAA town terminal; Cape Town Airport is 22km (14 miles) southeast of the city. A bus service runs to the railway station.

Domestic routes flown by South African Airways and a number of small independent airlines link the main cities and some smaller centres. Various private airlines operate flights to other towns and to Skukuza and Phalaborwa, serving Kruger National Park.

B

BUDGETING FOR YOUR TRIP

The following is an approximate guide to prices in South Africa.
Airport transfers. SAA bus from Johannesburg International Airport to central Johannesburg: R35, to Pretoria: R60; taxi to central Johannesburg R150 upwards; taxi from Cape Town International Airport to central Cape Town: R75–90.

Car hire. VW Polo: R250–325 per day. Minibus (VW Caravelle): R700–900 per day. Prices include collision damage waiver, other insurance and VAT. Prices are cheaper the longer the duration of hire.

Cigarettes. R12 (imported brands cost more).

Excursions. Full-day Cape Peninsula tour from Cape Town: R375–400; three-day Johannesburg–Kruger Park coach tour including most meals, entry fees and accommodation (shared room, per person): R3,050; three-day Johannesburg–Sun City coach tour including most meals and accommodation in double room: R2,400 per person.

Hairdressers. Man's haircut: R40–60 (tip expected); woman's haircut, shampoo, set and blow-dry: R100–150 (tip expected).

Hotels (double room with bath). 5-star: R1,500–3,500, 3-star: R600+ with breakfast, 1-star: R200+ with breakfast.

Meals and drinks (medium-priced restaurant). Lunch: R50–70; dinner: R80–120; bottle of wine: R70 upwards; beer: R7 upward; liquor R8 upward; soft drink: R5 upward.

National Parks. Entry fees: R60–120 per adult, R30–60 per child (under 12). Campsites: R100. Check the SANParks website for current tariffs: <www.sanparks.org>.

Petrol. R4.50 per litre.

Taxis. Fares vary from town to town. For safety, stick to metered taxis and avoid informal, mini-bus style cabs. Meters start at about R5, plus R2.50 per km (tip expected).

Trains (one way). Johannesburg–Cape Town, normal train: R450–650; Blue Train, standard compartment (per person, meals included): R18,300 upwards. Johannesburg–Pretoria: R30; Johannesburg–Durban: R200–300.

C

CAMPING AND CARAVANNING

Good weather and good roads account for the popularity of camping and caravanning in South Africa. There are about 650 caravan parks around the country, often in beautiful surroundings. Many have tent sites and amenities for campers too. Facilities at most sites are relatively lavish: hot and cold showers and bathrooms, laundries, rooms for ironing clothes and washing dishes and, in some cases, swimming pools, recreational halls, restaurants and shops. Popular parks, especially near the beaches, are likely to be full from mid-December to mid-January and at Easter.

You can rent a fully equipped caravan and the car to tow it, or, less widely available, a self-contained motor caravan (camper). Although hired cars can usually be picked up in one city and returned in another, caravans must go back to the point of hire if a collection charge is to be avoided.

CAR HIRE (See also DRIVING and BUDGETING FOR YOUR TRIP)

Some well-known international and local car-hire firms have offices at airports, in all big cities and even small towns throughout South Africa. The local companies usually have slightly lower tariffs. Cars offered are normally South African-built Japanese or German models, from two-door compacts with manual gearshift to big four-door automatics with air-conditioning. You need a valid driver's licence and usually a minimum age (23 or 25) is specified. A cash deposit may be required unless a recognised credit card is used for payment. Rates include basic insurance and sometimes collision damage waiver and personal accident insurance as well. There may be a per-kilometre charge. Fuel is not included. Rates will usually be lower if you reserve a car before arriving in South Africa, perhaps as part of a package booked through a travel agent. Chauffeur-driven cars are also available. As a rule, hire cars may not cross South Africa's borders.

CHILDREN

The young will take to the pools and beaches with glee, but pay attention to warnings about currents, jellyfish and other hazards.

You're advised to restrict the time children spend in the sun, especially at first, and to apply plenty of high-protection sun-screen.

CLIMATE

Arriving from the northern hemisphere, you'll find that the seasons are reversed south of the equator: July is mid-winter and Christmas can be hot. Winter nights can be cold, especially at higher altitudes – and that includes Johannesburg – though daytime temperatures are often delightful. In the parks and reserves game-spotting is easiest in winter (from July to October). Because it's dry then, there's much less foliage to afford cover to the animals.

	J	F	M	A	M	J	J	A	S	O	N	D
Cape Town												
°C Max	26	27	26	23	20	18	17	18	19	21	24	25
°F Max	79	80	79	74	68	64	63	64	66	70	75	77
°C Min	16	16	15	13	11	9	8	9	10	12	14	15
°F Min	61	61	59	55	52	48	46	48	50	54	57	59
Johannesburg												
°C Max	26	26	24	22	19	16	16	20	23	25	25	26
°F Max	79	79	75	72	66	61	61	68	74	77	77	79
°C Min	14	13	13	10	7	4	4	6	9	12	13	14
°F Min	57	55	55	50	45	39	39	43	48	54	55	57

CLOTHING

Even in summer, a degree of formality is appropriate after dark. A sign in your hotel may say: 'Gentlemen are requested to wear long trousers to dinner. Beachwear is not acceptable at any time in the restaurant.' In the more exclusive hotels and restaurants jackets and ties are recommended, though perhaps not obligatory.

At holiday resorts and while you're in transit, very casual clothing suffices. Fancy safari suits are quite unnecessary in the game parks; anything comfortable will do, though darker colours seem to attract fewer insects.

For South African summers, pack lightweight clothing, and a light jacket or sweater for the occasional chilly evening. A raincoat or umbrella also would be useful; summer is the rainy season in much of the country, though generally it's a matter of a passing thunderstorm to relieve the heat. (An exception is the Mediterranean-style Western Cape, which is dry all summer with rain in the winter.) On the Natal coast the Indian Ocean is swimmable all the year round.

CRIME AND SAFETY

As in much of the world, burglaries and muggings are commonplace in South African cities. Be prepared to find steel security gates and guards at restaurants, shops and car parks. It makes sense to lock your property out of sight in the boot of your car and always lock the doors. Use the hotel safe for any valuables. And don't go out flashing jewellery, walking alone at night, or otherwise inviting trouble.

CUSTOMS AND ENTRY REQUIREMENTS

Passport holders from the US, EU countries, Australia and New Zealand no longer require a visa to visit South Africa. However, as visa regulations are subject to change, it is wise to check with your travel agent or the nearest South African embassy or consulate. Alternatively, you can write to the Director General, Home Affairs: Private Bag X114, Pretoria 0001, South Africa; tel: 012-314 8911.

If you require a visa make sure you allow plenty of time for the application to be processed. If you plan to include a visit to any neighbouring countries and then return to South Africa, you should include this information on your application so that you receive a multiple-entry visa. Opening and closing times of border posts may be obtained by contacting the Department of Home Affairs, tel: 011-836 3228, fax: 011-834 6623.

On the plane, you'll be given a form to fill in. Present this on arrival to the Passport Control Officer, who will fix a temporary residence permit in your passport specifying the length and purpose of your stay. You may need to show a return ticket and some proof that you can support yourself in South Africa.

Here are the main items you may take into South Africa duty-free and, on your return home, into your own country:

	Cigarettes		Cigars		Tobacco	Spirits		Wine
S. Africa	*400*	*and*	*50*	*and*	*250g*	*1l*	*and*	*2l*
Australia	200	or	250g	or	250g	1l	or	1l
Canada	200	and	50	and	900g	1.1l	or	1.1l
Ireland	200	or	50	or	250g	1l	and	2l
N. Zealand	200	or	50	or	250g	1.1l	and	4.5l
UK	200	or	50	or	250g	1l	and	2l
US	200	and	100	and	*	1l	or	1l*

*A reasonable quantity.

Currency restrictions. Visitors may take any amount of foreign currency (travellers' cheques are obviously safer than cash) into South Africa. Large amounts should be declared upon arrival. The South African currency you may carry in or out is limited to R500.

D

DRIVING

With 73,500km (46,300 miles) of paved road, much of it excellent, South Africa is well suited for touring by car. There are some stretches of toll road, but the charges are quite modest. Away from the cities traffic is light and you can keep up high average speeds. Even dirt roads to more remote destinations are usually well graded.

Paperwork. You must have a valid driving licence with the details printed in English, or an accompanying certificate of authenticity in English, or an international licence, obtained before arrival in South Africa. To hire a car, there are no unusual requirements *(see page 105)*, but if you plan to import a car, advance planning and documentation are complicated. For details, consult the South Africa Tourism board *(see pages 123–4)* or the Automobile Association of South Africa: tel: 011-799 1000 or 0-800-010-101 (toll-free); <www.aasa.co.za>.

Driving conditions. As part of the British legacy, South Africa drives on the left. If you're not accustomed to it, start slowly and be especially vigilant when making turns. The speed limit on main highways is 120km/h (75mph). Elsewhere, the indicated limit may be 100km/h (62mph) or 80km/h (50mph) and you are generally restricted to 60km/h (37mph) in built-up areas unless otherwise posted. Driving standards are variable and the accident rate is high. In rural areas watch out for animals and pedestrians on the roads.

Police patrol cars are seen mostly near the cities and towns; if you break the law, you may be fined on the spot.

Road signs. Standard international pictographs are used for most situations, but there are some South African peculiarities. Printed signs are bilingual, for example, 'Border/Grens' or 'Ompad/Detour', or they alternate, so remember that Kaapstad means Cape Town. The frequently seen 'Slegs Only' with an arrow merely means the lane in question must only be used for turning. (*Slegs* means 'only' in Afrikaans.)

Parking restrictions are indicated by letters in circles painted on the road surface. Parking meters in most cities take a variety of coins.

'L' means loading zone (goods vehicles only); 'B' means reserved for buses, 'T' for taxis and 'FB' for fire-fighting equipment. 'S' with a diagonal stripe means no stopping, a striped 'P' is a no-parking indicator. Traffic lights are called 'robots' in English and Afrikaans.

Fuel. Filling stations are found on all main roads, although in country areas they're widely dispersed. Most filling stations are open 24 hours, seven days a week, but some stations in smaller towns may keep shorter hours, for instance from 7am until midnight. Grades of fuel available are 93 and 97 octane (but 87 and 93 in Johannesburg and the rest of the Witwatersrand because of the high altitude). Most stations offer full service and attendants are ready to clean the windscreen and check oil and water. Note: petrol cannot be purchased with credit cards.

Driving in the game parks and reserves. The Kruger National Park in particular is geared to the motor car, with about 900km (558 miles) of tarred roads, plus 1,500km (930 miles) of gravel roads. The speed limit is 50km/h (31mph) on tarred roads and 40km/h (25mph) on gravel, but slow driving gives animal pedestrians a better chance of survival, and you are more likely to sight game in the bush at 25km/h (15mph) – and on gravel or dirt roads you'll kick up much less dust.

Animals seem to consider the cars just another species of wildlife, but out of your car – even if you stick your head or arms out the window – you become a recognisable human, frightening some animals and prompting others to attack. This is why you must stay in the car anywhere beyond the fenced camps, barring an emergency. Park authorities emphasise that there are no tame animals, not even the lovable-looking vervet monkeys, which may bite. Feeding any animal is strictly forbidden.

Some more regulations: you may not drive off an authorised road into the bush or on to a road with a 'no entry' sign. Among other dangers, if your car should break down in an unauthorised place, help might not reach you for days. Any firearms must be declared and sealed at the gate. No pets are allowed.

One rule that is taken very seriously in the parks is the closing of the gates. In winter you must be back in your camp, or out of the park, by 5.30pm; in summer by 6.30pm. If you're five minutes late you'll be subject to a fine. The excuse that the road was blocked by elephants has been invented so often that it is no longer accepted, even when true. Night travel is forbidden in the national parks to protect animals and also to make life more difficult for poachers.

Bookings for any of the country's 20 national parks can be made through the SANParks website <www.sanparks.org>, or through the head office in Pretoria (tel: 012-428 9111). Another important conservation body is KZN (KwaZulu-Natal) Wildlife, which manages 66 reserves in Zululand, the Drakensberg and elsewhere in the province – online bookings at <www.kznwildlife.com> or ring 033-845 1000/1999.

E

ELECTRICITY

Voltage is generally 220/230 volts AC, 50 cycles (but Pretoria's is 250V). Plugs have three round pins. Hardware stores and supermarkets sell adapters for electric razors and other appliances.

EMBASSIES AND CONSULATES

(See also the *Yellow Pages* of local telephone directories under Consulates and Embassies.)

Australia: Mutual and Federal Building, 292 Orient Street, Arcadia, Pretoria; tel: 012-342 3740
14th floor, BP Centre, Long Street, Cape Town; tel: 021-419 5425

Canada: 1103 Arcadia Street, Hatfield, Pretoria; tel: 012-324 6923

Ireland: Delheim Suite, Tubach Centre, 1234 Church Street, Pretoria; tel: 012-342 5062

UK: 255 Hill Street, Arcadia, Pretoria; tel: 012-483 1200
1st Floor, Southern Life Centre, 8 Riebeeck Street, Cape Town; tel: 021-425 3670

UK (cont):   275 Jan Smuts Avenue, Dunkeld West,
                  Johannesburg; tel: 011-537 7000
                  19th floor, The Marine, 22 Gardiner Street, Durban;
                  tel: 031-305 3041
US: Thibault House, 877 Pretorius Street, Pretoria;
                  tel: 012-342 1048
                  Broadway Industries Centre, Heerengracht,
                  Cape Town; tel: 021-421 4280
                  1 River Street, Killarney, Jo'burg; tel: 011-644 8000

EMERGENCIES

Police: 10111
Ambulance: 999
Fire Brigade:
• Johannesburg: 999
• Cape Town: 535-1100
• Durban: 361-0000
Information (electronic *Yellow Pages*) for all towns/cities: 10118

G

GAY AND LESBIAN TRAVELLERS

The self-proclaimed gay capital of South Africa, Cape Town is the most amenable city in Africa for gay visitors. The tourist department produces an official 'pink map' listing gay and lesbian orientated guesthouses, night venues and facilities, and there is a helpline operating daily (tel: 021-4222 500). A pink map is also produced for Johannesburg and Pretoria. The Pink Route is a collection of gay-owned lodges and hotels through the Western Cape: <www.pinkroute.co.za>.

GETTING THERE

It's possible to go by container ship, cargo boat, or as part of a cruise, but most visitors fly. Although the fares and conditions described below have all been carefully checked, it is well worth consulting a travel agent for the latest information.

Scheduled flights. You can fly to South Africa from North America direct and via a number of European cities, including Athens, London, Frankfurt, Lisbon, Paris, Rome and Zurich.

There are non-stop flights from London Heathrow to Johannesburg, where a connecting service is offered to Cape Town, Durban, Port Elizabeth and other cities. Several airlines also operate direct services to Cape Town and Durban. You may also fly via one of South Africa's neighbours, perhaps making a stopover on the way.

The months of January, July and December are peak season for fares. April and May fares are lowest. Round the World (RTW) fares offered for certain routes include a stop in South Africa.

Charter flights and package tours

From North America: All-inclusive package tours are available. Costs covered include the round-trip airfare (usually from New York), accommodation, most or all meals, transfers, baggage handling, local transport and sightseeing.

From the UK: Tour operators offer a variety of holidays with everything included, as well as land-only packages if you wish to arrange your own air travel. Certain airlines can obtain hotel and car-hire discounts for their passengers. The South African Tourism board, *(see pages 123–4)*, gives information on tours and package holidays.

Some charter flights are currently offered to Johannesburg, but you must reserve far ahead as space fills up quickly.

GUIDES AND TOURS

City sightseeing tours and day excursions to beauty spots are normally led by bilingual (English and Afrikaans) guides. For interpreters of other languages, check with the local tourist office. Package tours of Kruger National Park are led by experienced guides who can help spot the animals and identify them. In the private game parks rangers are able to give attention to visitors' individual interests, such as bird-watching.

H

HEALTH AND MEDICAL CARE

Vaccinations. No vaccinations are required for entry into South Africa unless you are arriving from a yellow-fever zone, in which case you must have an international yellow-fever vaccination certificate.

Malaria preventative tablets should be taken by everyone planning to visit the lowveld of Mpumalanga or Limpopo Provinces (the Kruger Park or the private game parks nearby), Zululand in Natal, or certain areas of South Africa's neighbours. Ask your pharmacist or doctor to explain the precautions you must take. Or you can go to any pharmacy in South Africa and buy anti-malaria pills over the counter. Normally, you must start taking the pills several days before entering the affected district and continue the specified dosage for several weeks after leaving. A syrup is available for children.

As an additional precaution, try to avoid being bitten by mosquitoes, one variety of which is responsible for spreading the disease. Apply an insect repellent, cover up your skin outdoors after dusk, and keep mosquitoes out of your sleeping area, by using mosquito netting and/or air-conditioning.

Other problems. Apart from 'bluebottles' (men-of-war jellyfish) and tides, swimming in the ocean presents no special problems. However, you should be extremely careful about rivers and lakes: unless otherwise indicated, they may be inhabited by the dangerous bilharzia parasite, which can be contracted by ingesting unpurified water or through bare feet or skin in or near the water. Never drink from a river unless you've been assured its water is safe to drink.

Most of the 140 varieties of snake in South Africa are harmless, or almost, but if the worst happens, anti-snakebite serum is available.

Beware of the power of the sun. You can feel cool by the sea, or at higher altitudes, and still burn. Doctors recommend strict limits on exposure and using a sunscreen with a protection factor of at least 15.

Insurance. Since South Africa has no national health service, any medical treatment and hospitalisation must be paid for direct. If you have medical insurance already, make certain that it covers foreign countries. Otherwise, take out special travel insurance that includes coverage of accidents, illness, or hospitalisation on your trip.

Doctors. Most hotels have a list of nearby doctors in case of need. Or look in the white pages of the telephone directory under 'Mediese Praktisyns' or 'Medical Practitioners'.

Hospitals. All cities have well-equipped hospital facilities, some of international repute.

Pharmacies. In the big cities one pharmacy in each area stays open after normal business hours. Check in the local newspaper or at your hotel for details of late opening hours.

I

INTERNET

Internet facilities and email are widely available in most towns, both at tourist hotels and at internet cafés, but may not be found in game reserves and other more remote areas.

L

LANGUAGE

Since 1994, South Africa has recognised 11 official languages: English, Afrikaans, Zulu, Xhosa, Sotho, Venda, Tswana, Tsonga, Pedi, Shangaan and Ndebele. Most of the whites and people of mixed race (Coloureds) claim Afrikaans (derived from Dutch) as their mother tongue. In practice, you'll find most people understand English, but here are a few phrases you might try in an Afrikaans environment. Note that the 'g' is pronounced as a throaty 'kh', and 'oe' is pronounced 'oo'.

Good morning	**Goeie môre**
Good afternoon	**Goeie middag**
Good night	**Goeie nag**
Please	**Asseblief**
Thank you	**Dankie**
Goodbye	**Tot siens**

Many common Afrikaans words and expressions have been borrowed by English-speakers in South Africa. Here are some distinctive words that you might hear:

bakkie	pickup truck
braai	barbecue
combi	microbus or minibus
dorp	small town
kop/koppie	hilltop/small hill
rondavel	circular hut/house
robot	traffic light
tsotsi	mugger, street criminal

M

MAPS

South African Tourism *(see pages 123–4)* issues (free) excellent tourist maps of South Africa and the regions. Local information offices, car-hire firms and the Automobile Association (for AA members) are also sources of free maps. Extremely detailed, indexed maps of cities and regions are sold at bookstores.

MONEY MATTERS

Currency. The unit of currency of South Africa is the rand (R), divided into 100 cents (c). For currency restrictions, *see page 108.*

Coins: 1c and 2c (both are being phased out), 5c, 10c, 20c and 50c; R1, R2 (a small coin, easily mistaken for one of lesser value) and R5.

Banknotes: R10, R20, R50, R100 and R200. The R200 note looks a lot like the R20, so be alert.

Banking hours. Monday to Friday 9am–3.30pm, Saturday 8.30am–11am (later in major cities). Small-town banks may close for lunch from 12.45pm–2pm (except Wednesday and Saturday).

Credit cards and travellers' cheques. All commercial banks cash travellers' cheques in any major hard currency. Many hotels and shops also welcome travellers' cheques. Major international credit cards are accepted in most hotels, many shops and by tour operators and carriers. Some bank branches will advance cash against a major credit card. Cash machines (ATMs) are available in major cities and towns for those on the Cirrus and Plus systems.

Taxes. VAT at a standard rate (currently 14 percent) is charged on all purchases of goods and services, except on some basic foodstuffs. It is included in the prices advertised. VAT may be reclaimed when the total value of items taken out of the country exceeds R250. For information on the refund process, contact the VAT Refund Administrators, P.O. Box 107, Johannesburg International Airport Post Office, 1627; tel: 011-394 1117.

O

OPENING HOURS

Business hours are typically 8.30am–4.30pm. Most shops are open Mon–Fri 8.30am–6pm, Sat until 12.30pm. Some greengrocers, pharmacies, bookshops and supermarkets may stay open later. Cafés (essentially small general stores) may operate seven days a week 6am–midnight. Some big shopping centres stay open until 5pm on Saturday and until lunchtime on Sunday, others like Cape Town's V&A Waterfront open 9am–9pm, even on Sunday. Beachfront shops of all kinds in Durban stay open all day on Sunday.

P

PHOTOGRAPHY

Some, but not all, international brands of film are on sale. Sameday colour printing is available in most cities and larger resorts. Keep your film as cool as possible in the semi-tropical regions. Never leave your camera locked in a car parked in the hot sun.

It's worth taking plenty of spare batteries, particularly if you are using a digital camera. Rechargeable batteries can be topped up at hotels and lodges. If you've just bought a new camera, taking some test pictures before you leave home. Check that your travel insurance covers your equipment.

Photographing wildlife requires fast film – at least ISO 200 – because the subject may move, and so may your long lens. Even if you don't have a telephoto or zoom lens, many animals come so close that you can still get some good pictures.

POLICE (See also EMERGENCIES)

Members of the national police force, who are armed, wear blue uniforms and peaked caps. In the cities they usually drive small 'Black Maria' vans (actually yellow) with caged space for culprits. The traffic police wear khaki uniforms.

POST OFFICES

Most post offices are open Mon–Fri 8.30am–4.30pm, Sat 8am–noon. Smaller offices close for lunch from 1–2pm.

They deal with a complicated variety of services, from issuing television licences to dealing with pensions, so you may have to wait for your postage stamps. Mail boxes, many of them bearing the monograms of British sovereigns, are painted red. Service is reasonably fast for overseas mail.

Poste restante. If you're not sure where you'll be staying, you may have mail addressed to you *poste restante* (general delivery). The main post offices – on Parliament Street in Cape Town, West Street in Durban, Jeppe Street in Johannesburg and Church Square in Pretoria – have special counters for this service.

Telegrams. The post office handles electronic communications as well. Any branch office will accept your telegram. The main post offices in Johannesburg and Cape Town have a cable and telegraph counter available 24 hours a day.

PUBLIC HOLIDAYS

January 1	New Year's Day
March 21	Human Rights' Day
April 27	Freedom Day
May 1	Workers' Day
June 16	Youth Day
August 9	National Women's Day
September 24	Heritage Day
December 16	Day of Reconciliation
December 25/26	Xmas Day/Goodwill Day

Movable dates:
Good Friday, Family Day (Easter Monday).

PUBLIC TRANSPORT

Buses. In Johannesburg the Publicity Association sells reduced-rate tickets for unlimited travel on the buses except at peak hours. Bus-route maps and timetables are also sold at the City Hall, Market Street. Evening services are sparse, and from 2pm on Saturday until

Monday morning all municipal buses depart from the station at Main and Rissik streets.

Bus services in other cities are less complex – local information offices will help. In all buses, even the double-deckers, you pay the driver on the way in. Keep your ticket, as an inspector is likely to board the bus to double check.

Trains. Many South African trains are fascinating. Hundreds of steam locomotives still earn their keep – a thrill for train buffs. –Several narrow-gauge lines still operate, including the Apple Express west from Port Elizabeth to Avontuur – 285km (177 miles) of 61-cm (2-ft) gauge railway. At the other end of the scale the Blue Train *(see page 80)*, the pride of South African Railways, maintains five-star luxury between Pretoria and Cape Town. All long-distance trains have sleeping compartments in first and second class. Daily commuter trains are far less glamorous.

R

RADIO AND TELEVISION

There has been a veritable explosion of new radio stations following a new system brought in to replace the apartheid-era monopoly of radio by the South African Broadcasting Corporation (SABC). There are now some 65 community stations representing a wide spectrum of interests, from universities to religious and ethnic groupings. Meanwhile, the SABC transmits various services on FM, including the English Service – a mix of news, music and features; the Afrikaans Service; and Radio 5, which specialises in pop music. In addition, there are regional services (strong on pop) on AM and FM, and stations broadcasting in the major black languages. BBC, Voice of America and European shortwave stations can be picked up; BBC and VOA also use a medium-wave frequency for southern Africa.

The state-run SABC operates three public television channels, all of which show a mix of local and international sitcoms, game shows, dramas and old films, as well as broadcasting news, sporting events and opinion programs. The only private non-subscribers channel ETV offers up a similar mix. Many hotels also have M-Net, a subscribers-only channel showing more recent films, together with its multi-channel satellite subsidiary DSTV, which includes several sports and movie channels, as well as the likes of CNN, BBC World, Sky TV and MTN.

T

TAXIS

In South African cities the taxis do not normally cruise for fares. You must go to a taxi rank or ask your hotel desk clerk to call a cab by phone. In Johannesburg taxis are usually found outside the Carlton Centre in Kruis Street. In Cape Town a likely taxi rank is opposite the Air Terminal in Lower Adderley Street. The word taxi also applies to the many minibuses which ply fixed routes.

TELEPHONES

South Africa's automatic network functions efficiently, and you can dial direct to many other countries. The international access code is 09. (The country code to use in IDD calls to South Africa is 27.)

Calls within South Africa are cheaper between 6pm and 8pm from Monday to Friday and cheapest between 8pm and 7am, and from 1pm on Saturday to 7am on Monday.

Coin-operated telephones in street boxes, cafés, and public places take 20c, 50c, R1, R2 and R5 coins. Directions are given in English and Afrikaans. Phone cards in R10 denominations are available at post offices and other outlets. They can be used at green public telephones for calls within South Africa and international calls. In Johannesburg an international telephone office on the ground floor of the Post Office building in Smal Street is open 24 hours a day. Mobile phones are extremely popular and can be hired at Johannesburg International Airport. For local directory assistance, tel: 1023; national directory assistance, tel: 1025.

TIME DIFFERENCES

All year round, South Africa stays on GMT + 2. For example, during (northern) winter:

Los Angeles	New York	London	**South Africa**	Sydney
2am	5am	10am	**noon**	9pm

TIPPING

In South Africa tipping is less generous than in most of Europe and North America. Tips are expected, but not always received, by filling station attendants, hotel maids, railway porters, taxi drivers, waiters, stewards and caddies.
Some suggestions:

Hairdresser	10 percent
Maid, per week	R20–25
Porter, per bag	R5
Taxi driver	10 percent
Tour guide	10 percent
Waiter	10 percent if service charge is not included

TOURIST INFORMATION

For local information, all larger towns and cities have a Tourist Information Bureau, which can be identified by a large white 'I' on a green background, and will be able to provide city maps, information on current events, museums and other points of interest. For research in advance, the country's nine provincial authorities all have excellent websites that generally include links to more local sources of tourist information within the province.

Contact details for the provinces are as follows:

Eastern Cape Tourism: tel: 043-701 9600, fax: 043-701 9649, email: info@ectourism.co.za, <www.ectourism.co.za>

Free State Tourism Marketing Board: tel: 051-403 3719, fax: 051-403 3718, <www.freestateprovince.co.za>

Gauteng Tourism Agency: tel: 011-340 9000, email: tourism@gauteng.net, <www.gauteng.net>

KwaZulu-Natal Tourism Authority: tel: 031-366 7500, fax: 031-6693, email: tkzn@iafrica.com, <www.kzn.org.za>

Limpopo Tourism Board: tel: 015-290 7300, fax: 015-291 4140, email: info.limpopo@mweb.co.za, <www.tourismboard.co.za>

Mpumalanga Tourism Authority: tel: 013-752 7001, email: mtanlpsa@cis.co.za, <www.mpumalanga.com>

Northern Cape Tourism Authority: tel: 053-832 1434, <www.northerncape.org.za>

North-West Parks and Tourism Authority: tel: 018-386 1225, email: epholo@nwpq.org.za, <www.tourismnorthwest.co.za>

Western Cape Tourism Board: tel: 021-483 9181, fax: 021-483 9182, email: info@capetourism.org, <www.capetourism.org>

Each main centre also has an office run by South African Tourism. This will be able to provide countrywide information, including brochures, maps and accommodation details. The main office in Johannesburg is very helpful and able to answer most enquiries. Addresses and telephone and fax numbers are given on all major South African Tourism publications.

The head office postal address is:

Private Bag: X10012, Sandton 2146; tel: 011-778 8000, fax: 011-778 8001, <www.southafrica.net>

South African Tourism offices abroad:

Australia   Level 1, 117 York Street, Sydney NSW 2000;
tel: 02-9621 5000, fax: 02-9261 200.

UK	6 Alt Grove, Wimbledon, London SW19 4DZ; tel: 020-8971 9364 or 08701 550044, fax: 020-8944 6705
US	500 Fifth Avenue, 20th Floor, New York, NY 10110; tel: 212-730 2929 or 800-593 1318, fax: 212-760 1980
	6300 Wilshire Boulevard, Suite 600, Los Angeles, CA90048; tel: 323-651 0902, fax: 323-651 5969

TRAVELLERS WITH DISABILITIES

Great advances have been made in recent years in the provision of special toilet facilities and wheelchair access to public buildings, hotels and other places visitors might want to go. South African Tourism's accommodation brochure *(see page 102)*, gives details of these facilities, and the Independent Living Institute, <www.independentliving.org>, can also advise you on specific facilities and services.

W

WATER

You can drink tap water anywhere in South Africa – even in the game parks. In some coastal areas it may be tinted by iron deposits, but it's still potable.

WEBSITES

Useful websites covering South Africa include the following:
• <www.africa-geographic.com> News and features from a leading wildlife and ecological magazine.
• <www.anc.org.za> The official mouthpiece of the ANC has plenty of coverage of contemporary issues.
• <www.coastingafrica.com> Comprehensive coverage of South Africa's backpacker hostels and related facilities.

• <www.getawaytoafrica.com> Website of South Africa's most popular travel magazine.
• <www.iafrica.com> Current news and features by a leading local internet provider.
• <www.mg.co.za> The *Mail & Guardian* newspaper online.
• <www.platterwineguide.co.za> Online version of Platter's popular wine guide.
• <www.sanparks.org> Information and booking facilities for the country's 20 national parks.
• <www.southafrica.co.za> Useful general site with up-to-date information about weather, exchange rates and tourist attractions, as well as good maps.
• <www.southafrica.net> Official site of South African Tourism.
• <www.struikpublishers.co.za> Publisher of more than 100 books covering South Africa's scenery, wildlife and cultures.
• <www.sundaytimes.co.za> Good news and sport coverage.
• <www.womensnet.org.za> News and links for women's issues in South Africa.

WEIGHTS AND MEASURES

South Africa uses the metric system.

Y

YOUTH AND BACKPACKER HOSTELS

For full information, check out the website of Hostelling International South Africa (HISA), <www.hisa.org.za>, or contact them at St George's House, 3rd floor, 73 St George's Mall, Cape Town 8001; tel: 021-424 2511, fax: 021-424 4119. The last 10 years has seen a burgeoning growth in the number of private hostels and other facilities catering mainly to backpackers. Most are listed and reviewed in the free booklet *Coast to Coast* and related website <www.coastingafrica.com>.

Recommended Hotels

In the following pages we offer a short selection of establishments in the areas covered in the Where to Go section of this book (and in the same order). The list is by no means exhaustive, but is designed to give you a few pointers by selecting places which offer something extra in the way of facilities, location, character, or value for money. For a brief guide to the camps in the Kruger National Park, *see page 41*.

Our ratings are an indication of the cost per person, sharing a double room, with breakfast. Many country retreats and game lodges only publish rates for dinner, bed and breakfast, however. Note that there may be very wide seasonal variations, and these prices are only approximate as the rapid inflation of recent years seems likely to continue.

$$$$	R1,500–R3,000
$$$	R600+
$$	R250+
$	R200+

GAUTENG

JOHANNESBURG

The Grace $$$$ *54 Bath Ave, Rosebank 2196; tel: 011-280 7200; fax: 011-280 7474; <www.thegrace.co.za>*. Luxury country-house-style hotel with handy location for the shopping and nightlife facilities of Rosebank. Rooftop pool and garden, gym, parking. 73 rooms.

Intercontinental Sandton Sun and Towers Johannesbsurg $$$$ *Corner Fifth Street and Alice Lane, PO Box 784902, Sandton 2146; tel: 011-780 5000; fax: 011-780 5002; <www.ichotels group.com>*. Opulent modern tower adjoining a vast shopping complex. Glittering interior, pool, sauna, gardens, health club, cocktail lounge, parking. 564 rooms.

Mercure Inn Randburg Waterfront $$ *Corner Republic and Randburg streets, Randburg Waterfront, Johannesburg 2125; tel: 011-762 4308; fax: 011-762 4491.* Comfortable budget hotel close to excellent shopping and entertainment facilities. 104 rooms.

The Saxon $$$$ *36 Saxon Road, Sandhurst, Sandton, tel: 011-292 6000; fax: 011-292 6001; <www.thesaxon.com>.* Prestigious hideout favoured by Nelson Mandela, with high-class decor and cuisine, and rooms the size of aircraft hangars.

Sunnyside Park $$$ *2 York Road, Parktown, Johannesburg 2193; tel: 011-643 7226; fax: 011-642 0019; <www.legacyhotels.co.za>.* Gracious former residence of the British High Commissioner, situated in a park and garden setting. Pool. 100 rooms.

Town Lodge $$$ *Herman Road, Harmelia Ext 2, Germiston; tel: 011-974 5202; fax: 011-974 7126; email: <tljia.resv@citylodge. co.za>.* Just 5km (3 miles) from Jo'burg Airport. Airport shuttle bus service. Air-conditioned rooms with TV and shower. 135 rooms.

The Westcliff $$$$ *67 Jan Smuts Avenue, Westcliff 2193; tel: 011-646 2400; fax: 011-646 3500; <www.westcliff.co.za>.* Luxurious modern hotel perched on a ridge and enjoying spectacular views over the city. Pool, health club. 115 rooms.

PRETORIA

Arcadia $$ *515 Proes Street, Pretoria 0083; tel: 012-326 9311; fax: 012-326 1067; <www.arcadiahotel.co.za>.* A centrally located modern block attached to a shopping mall. 139 rooms.

Crowne Plaza Holiday Inn $$$$ *Church Street/Beatrix Street, PO Box 40694, Pretoria 0007; tel: 012-341 1571; fax: 012-440-7534.* Centrally located for government offices and cultural attractions. Pool, entertainment. 241 rooms.

Pretoria Hof Hotel $$$ *Pretorius/Van der Walt streets, Pretoria 0002; tel: (012) 322-7570; fax: (012) 322-9461.* Modern hotel in the city centre, offering a range of business facilities and entertainment. 116 rooms.

Sheraton Pretoria Hotel & Towers $$$$ *Corner Church and Wessels streets, Arcadia; tel: 012-429 9999; fax: 012-429 9300; <www.sheraton.com>.* Probably the largest hotel in the city centre and the only one approaching five-star standards. 175 rooms.

SUN CITY

Kwa Maritane Bush Lodge $$$ *Pilanesburg National Park, Sun City 0316; tel: 014-552-5100; fax: 014-552 5333; <www.legacy hotels.co.za>.* Game lodge in Pilanesburg Park, adjacent to Sun City. Pools, tennis, children's playground. 25 chalets and 28 cabanas.

The Palace of the Lost City $$$$ *PO Box 308, Sun City 0316; tel: 014-557 1000; reservations: 011-780 7800; <www.suninternational. com>.* Extravagant hotel set in the vast, exotic resort of Sun City, which features casino, health centre, pools, golf, tennis. 338 rooms.

MADIKWE GAME RESERVE

Mosetlha Bush Camp $$$ *PO Box 78690, Sandton 2146; tel: 011-444 9345 or 083-653 9869; <www.thebushcamp.com>.* This rustic unfenced bush camp accommodates a maximum of 16 people in 9 double cabins.

Tau Game Lodge $$$$ *PO Box 1450, Halfwayhouse 1685; tel: 011-314 4350; fax: 011-314 1162; <www.taugamelodge.com>.* Built in 1995, this classy lodge consists of 30 thatched chalets set in a semi-circle around a vast natural waterhole that attracts a variety of game.

MPUMALANGA AND LIMPOPO PROVINCES

Casa do Sol $$$ *PO Box 57, Hazyview; tel: 013-737 8111; fax: 013-737 8116; <wwwcasadosol.co.za>.* Village of villas and cottages in woodlands. Pools, tennis, riding, fishing, game reserve. 40 rooms.

The Chestnut Country Lodge $$$ *PO Box 156, Kiepersol, Hazyview 1241; tel: 013-737 8195; fax: 013-737 8196; <www.chestnutlodge.co.za>*. Farmstead, suites and cottages in lush gardens and farmland. Pool, bird-watching. Close to Kruger's Numbi Gate.

Hazyview Protea $$$$ *On the R40 road, Burgershall, Hazyview 1242; tel: 013-737 7332; fax: 013-737 7335; <www.proteahotels. com>*. Short drive from the Kruger National Park and several private reserves. Set in large gardens with fine views. Pool, tennis. 92 rooms.

Hulala Lakeside Lodge $$$ *PO Box 1382, White River 1240; tel: 013-764 1893: fax: 013-764 1864; <www.hulala.co.za>*. Country-house hotel by lake. Pool. Bird-watching, fishing, windsurfing, canoeing on the lake. 25 rooms.

Londolozi Game Reserve $$$$ *Sabi Sand Reserve, PO Box 6, Skukuza 1350; reservations through CC Africa, tel: 011-809 4300; fax: 011-809 4400; <www.ccafrica.com>*. Known for its top-range quality, comfort and service. Escorted drives/walks in bush. Highly rated for leopard sightings. Four private camps and one safari lodge.

MalaMala Game Reserve $$$$ *Sabi Sand Reserve, via Skukuza 1353, PO Box 55514, Northlands 2116; tel: 031-765 2900; reservations: 011-442 2267; <www.malamala.com>*. Luxurious game lodge, with chalets in an idyllic setting. Experienced game rangers on staff.

Motswari Game Lodge $$$$ *Timbavati Game Reserve, PO Box 67865, Bryanston 2021; tel: 011-463 1990; fax: 011-463 1992; <www.motswari.co.za>*. 15 luxury rondavels, pool. The game reserve is adjacent to the Kruger National Park.

Mount Sheba Country Lodge $$$ *above Pilgrim's Rest, PO Box 100, Pilgrim's Rest 1290; tel: 013-768 1241; fax: 013-768 1248; <www.mountsheba.co.za>*. 25 rooms in own nature reserve. Hilltop and forest setting, thatched stone houses. Pool, walks, bird-watching.

Ngala Game Lodge $$$$ *Timbavati Game Reserve; reservations through CC Africa, tel: 011-809 4300; fax: 011-809 4400;*

<www.ngala.co.za>. 20 luxury thatched chalets, pool. Rangers escort walks and drives through the bush.

Sabi River Sun $$$$ *Main Sabie Road, PO Box 13, Hazyview 1242; tel: 013-737 7311; fax: 013-737 7314; <www.southernsun. com>.* Luxury hotel located close to the Kruger National Park. Fishing, swimming pool, bowling green, squash and tennis courts.

Sabi Sabi Game Reserve $$$$ *Sabi Sand Reserve, Skukuza 1350; tel: 011-483 3939; fax: 011-483 3799; <www.sabisabi.com>.* Luxury lodges amid big-game area bordering Kruger National Park. Pools. Rangers take you on day and night safaris. 46 rooms.

Singita Boulders Lodge $$$$ *Sabi Sand Reserve; tel: 011-784 7077; fax: 011-784 7667; <www.singita.co.za>.* Nine luxury suites, each with pool.

Thornybush Game Reserve $$$$ *Near Hoedspruit; tel: 011-883 7918/9; fax: 011-883 8201; <www.thornybush.co.za>.* Beautifully appointed thatched chalets and pool overlook bush near Kruger Park. Day and night walks escorted by rangers. Wide range of game.

DRAKENSBERG

Ardmore Guest Farm $$ *PO Box 122, Champagne Valley, Winterton 3340; tel: 036-468 1314; fax: 036-468 1241; <www. ardmore.co.za>.* Small owner-managed guesthouse lying on grassy green farmland overshadowed by the peaks of Champagne Castle. Superb home-cooked four-course meals; reasonably priced.

Cathedral Peak Hotel $$$ *Near Winterton, KwaZulu-Natal 3340; tel: 036-488 1888; fax: 036-488 1889; <www.cathedral peak.co.za>.* Resort and a fine base for walking and exploring in the Drakensberg. Thatched cottages and suites, pool, tennis, bowls, squash, riding and fishing. 90 rooms.

Champagne Sports Resort $$$ *Private Bag X9, Winterton 3340; tel: 036-468 1088; fax: 036-468 1072; <www.champagne*

sportsresort.com>. Hotel and thatched cottages in mountain scenery. Tennis, bowls, squash, riding, golf, pool. 62 hotel rooms.

Orion Mont-Aux-Sources Hotel $$$ *Private bag X1670, Bergville, KwaZulu-Natal 3350; tel: 036-438 8000; reservations: 0861 99199; fax: 036-438 6201; <www.orion-hotels.co.za>*. Situated at the entrance to Royal Natal National Park, arguably the most scenic setting in the Drakensberg, this quiet hotel has good sports facilities and hiking possibilities. 107 rooms.

Sandford Park Lodge $$$ *PO Box 7, Bergville, KwaZulu-Natal 3350; tel: 036-448 1001; fax: 036-448 1047*. Resort in garden and woodland setting in Drakensberg foothills. Pool, riding, bowls, fishing, bird-watching. 26 rooms.

DURBAN AND KWAZULU-NATAL COAST

Blue Marlin $$ *PO Box 24, Scottburgh 4180; tel: 039-978 3361; fax: 039-976 0971; <www.bluemarlin.co.za>*. Resort on south coast. 120 en-suite rooms.

Holiday Inn Durban Elangeni $$$$ *63 Snell Parade, Durban 4000; tel: 031-362 1300; fax: 031-332 5527*. Towering, luxury hotel with ocean views and very close to the beach. Pools. 447 rooms.

Oyster Box Hotel $$$$ *2 Lighthouse Road, Umhlanga Rocks, Natal 4320; tel: 031-561 2233; fax: 031-561 4072; <www.oyster box.co.za>*. On the beach, amid tropical gardens, in sight of Umhlanga lighthouse, with pool, tennis and fishing. 88 rooms.

Protea Hotel Edward $$$ *149 Marine Parade, Durban 4000; tel: 031-337 3681; fax: 031-332 1692; <www.proteahotels.com>*. Classic white block on the Golden Mile seafront. 101 rooms.

The Royal Hotel $$$$ *267 Smith Street, Durban 4000; tel: 031-333 6000; fax: 031-333 6002; <www.theroyal.co.za>*. Large, old, established and fully modernised luxury hotel in city centre. Pool, squash, health club. Many restaurants. 251 rooms.

ZULULAND

Hilltop Camp $$ *Hluhluwe Game Reserve; tel: 035-562 0848; reservations: 033-845-1000; <www.kznwildlife.com>.* Modern motel-like rest camp with 65 en-suite chalets and huts offering expansive views across green hills dotted with wildlife.

Kingfisher Lodge $$ *187 McKenzie Street, PO Box 291, St Lucia Village 3936; tel/fax: 035-590 1015; email: <stluciakingfisherlodge @mweb.co.za>.* Smart seven-room B&B set in lush gardens on St Lucia Estuary – great for birds, hippos and duikers.

Kwa-Bhekithunga $$$ *Stewart's Farm, PO Box 364, Eshowe 3815; tel: 035-460 0644; fax: 035-460 0867.* Low-key family-run lodge offering cosy accommodation in beehive huts and a cultural programme that places substance over style.

Mpila Camp $$ *Imfolozi Game Reserve; tel: 035-550 8476/7.* Rustic self-catering camp whose elevated safari tents regularly receive nocturnal visits from spotted hyena, porcupine and other small carnivores. No restaurant, and the small shop has limited supplies.

Ondoni Cultural Museum $$ *PO Box 523, Ulundi 3838; tel: 035-870 2051 or 2054; email: <amafahq@mweb.co.za>.* Budget beehive huts on the site of the Zulu King Cetshwayo's last *kraal*.

Phinda Resource Reserve $$$$ *near Mkhuze, Natal; reservations through CC Africa, tel: 011-809 4300; fax: 011-809 4400; <www.ccafrica.com>.* Five luxury Big Five game lodges in river and forest settings, offering 4x4 excursions and walking safaris.

Shakaland $$$$ *PO Box 103, Eshowe 3815; tel: 035-460 0912; fax: 035-460 0824; <www.shakaland.com>.* Commodious en-suite traditional beehive huts with air-con complement an excellent Zulu cultural programme that starts at 4pm for overnight visitors.

Simunye $$$$ *PO Box 248 Melmoth 3835; tel: 035-450 3111; fax: 035-450 2534.* This fabulously down-to-earth lodge also has a great Zulu cultural programme, starting at 3.30pm, when visitors are transported by ox-cart from a meeting point on the R66.

Zulu Nyala Lodge $$$ *PO Box 163, Hluhluwe 3960; tel: 035-562 0169; fax: 035-562 0646; <www.zulunyala.com>*. This private game reserve adjacent to Phinda supports many of the same species. Luxury tented camps, including guided 4x4 drives and good food.

EASTERN CAPE AND GARDEN ROUTE

Bitou River Lodge $$$ *PO Box 491, Plettenberg Bay 6600; tel/fax: 044-535 9577; <www.bitou.co.za>*. Voted South Africa's Best B&B/ Guest House in 2003, this luxurious owner-managed lodge consists of just five rooms set along the forested banks of the Bitou River – canoes available – about 10km (6 miles) from Plettenberg Bay.

Eight Bells Mountain Inn $$$ *PO Box 436, Mossel Bay 6500; tel: 044-631 0000; fax: 044-631 0004; <www.eightbells.co.za>*. Family-run country inn set amid stunning mountain scenery halfway between Mossel Bay and Oudtshoorn. Wide variety of sports facilities.

The Plettenberg $$$$ *40 Church Street, PO Box 719, Plettenberg Bay 6600; tel: 044-533 2030; fax: 044-533 2074; <www.plettenberg. com>*. Luxurious resort overlooking the sea. Pool. 38 rooms.

Protea Hotel Edward $$$ *Belmont Terrace, Port Elizabeth 6001; tel: 041-586 2056; fax: 041-586 4925; <www.proteahotels.com>*. Centrally located in historic district, overlooking the bay. 110 rooms.

Shamwari Game Reserve $$$$ *PO Box 113, Swartkops, Port Elizabeth 6210; tel: 042-203 1111; fax: 042-235 1224; <www. shamwari.com>*. Award-winning private game reserve near Addo, with superior accommodation inclusive of guided game drives that offer the opportunity to see the Big Five and African wild dogs.

Tsitsikamma Lodge $$$ *N2 National Road, Storms River 6308; tel: 042-280 3802; fax: 042-280 3803; <www.tsitsikamma.com>*. Award-winning hunting lodge. Base for Tsitsikamma National Parks.

CAPE TOWN AND CAPE PENINSULA

Alphen $$$–$$$$ *Alphen Drive, PO Box 35, Constantia, Cape Town 7848; tel: 021-794 5011; fax: 021-794 5710.* Magnificent historic estate in beautiful setting. Pool, sports centre with tennis, squash. 34 rooms.

The Cellars-Hohenort $$$ *93 Brommersvlei Road, Constantia, Cape Town 7800; tel: 021-794 2137; fax: 021-794 2149; <www. cellars-hohenort.com>.* Graceful hotel converted from the 18th-century cellars of the former Klaasenbosch wine farm. Set in large landscaped gardens. Two pools, tennis, golf. Close to Kirstenbosch.

Lord Nelson Inn $$ *58 St George's Street, False Bay, Simonstown 7795; tel: 021-786 1386; fax: 021-786 1009; email: <nsnelson@ mweb.co.za>.* Reasonably priced inn-like hotel with an agreeable location in Simonstown and just 10 rooms.

Majoro's Bed and Breakfast $$ *69 Helena Crescent, Graceland, Khayelitsha, Cape Town; tel: 021-361 3412; <www. tiscover.co.za/majoros.* Traditional African experience, complete with trip to a local township *shebeen.* Cash only.

Mount Nelson $$$$ *76 Orange Street, Cape Town 8001; tel: 021-483 1000; fax: 021-483 1782; <www.mountnelson.co.za>.* Celebrated luxury hotel in spacious gardens. Pools, gym, tennis, squash. 201 rooms.

The Peninsula $$$$ *313 Beach Road, Sea Point, Cape Town 8061; tel: 021-430 7777; fax: 021-430 7776; <www.peninsula.co.za>.* Suites, many with spa baths, overlooking seafront. Pool. 110 rooms.

Twelve Apostles Hotel $$$$ *About 2km (1¼ miles) south of Camps Bay; tel: 021-437 9051; fax: 021-437 9055; <www. 12apostleshotel.com>.* Since it opened in 2003, this boutique hotel has been hot-listed in *Condé Nast Traveller* and *Travel and Leisure,* while *GQ* named it 'Hotel with the Best View in the World' – with food, service and ambience to match.

Victoria & Alfred Hotel $$$ *The Pierhead, The Waterfront, PO Box 50050, Vlaeberg, Cape Town 8002; tel: 021-419 6677; fax: 021-419 8955; <www.vahotel.co.za>.* Elegant hotel in dockside redevelopment area. Spacious, air-conditioned rooms, with ensuite bathroom and wi-fi internet access. 68 rooms.

The Vineyard Hotel and Spa $$$–$$$$ *Colinton Road (off Protea Road), PO Box 151, Newlands, Cape Town 7725; tel: 021-657 4500; fax: 021-657 4501.* Beautifully restored country-house hotel in landscaped gardens, Health and fitness centre. 173 rooms.

CAPE WINELANDS

Cathbert Country Inn $$$ *On the R44 between Paarl and Franschhoek, Simondium, PO Box 3425, Paarl 7620; tel: 021-874 1366; fax: 021-874 3918; <www.cathbert.co.za>.* In the foothills of the Simonsberg mountains, just 40 minutes from Cape Town. Suites with verandahs and secluded garden.

The D'Ouwe Werf $$ *30 Church Street, Stellenbosch 7600; tel: 021-887 4608; fax: 021-887 4626; <www.ouwewerf.com>* Elegantly restored old country inn. Pool, gardens. 31 en-suite rooms.

Grande Roche $$$$ *Plantasie Street, PO Box 6038, Paarl 7620; tel: 021-863 2727; fax: 021-863 2220; <www.granderoche.com>.* Former historic Cape Dutch farm buildings converted into luxury suites. Pools, tennis, gym, outdoor theatre.

NORTH AND NORTHWESTERN CAPE PROVINCE

Holiday Inn Garden Court Kimberley $$$ *120 Du Toitspan Road, PO Box 635, Kimberley 8300; tel: 053-831 1751; fax: 053-831 1814; <www.ichotelsgroup.com>.* Luxurious resort and business hotel. Pool, sauna, fitness centre. 135 rooms.

Waterwiel Lodge $$ *Voortrekker Street, Kakamas 8870; tel: 054-431 0838; fax: 054-431 0836.* Small resort in the vicinity of the Augrabies Falls National Park. Pool, tennis. 25 rooms.

Recommended Restaurants

Here we can give only a small selection from the wide range of different eating places found in the major cities and suburbs. We don't cover the small towns and country areas, where it is usual to eat at wherever you are staying: the hotels and game lodges have their own, often very good, restaurants *(see pages 126–35)*.

When you telephone for a reservation, you can ask if the restaurant is licensed to sell wine, and if not, whether you may bring your own.

As a rough guide to prices, we have marked each entry with one, two or three $ symbols. These correspond to the approximate cost of a three-course dinner per person, not including drinks, as follows:

$$$	over R250
$$	R120–250
$	up to R120

JOHANNESBURG AND ENVIRONS

Le Canard $$$ *163 Rivonia Road, Morningside, Sandton; tel: 011-884 4597.* Award-winning French and international cuisine in a gracious house and garden setting. Also with a notable wine list.

The Carnivore $$ *Muldersdrift Estate, Muldersdrift; tel: 011-957 2099.* Vast carvery where the meat (mostly game) is spit-roasted over a huge charcoal fire in the middle of the restaurant. It's wise to build up an appetite for a few days before coming here.

Daruma $$$ *Intercontinental Sandton Sun and Towers Hotel, corner Fifth Street and Alice Lane, Sandton; tel: 011-780 5000.* Long regarded as *the* Japanese restaurant in town, Daruma serves a full range of traditional dishes. Reservations essential.

Dinos $$ *Bedford Centre, near Bruma Lake; tel: 011-622 3007.* Stylish continental cuisine with a good range of game and fish dishes.

Gramadoelas at the Market $$ *Market Theatre Precinct, Wolhuter Street, Newtown, Johannesburg; tel: 011-838 6960.* A magnet for overseas visitors who come for the superb South African cuisine, including such delicacies as crocodile.

Ile de France $$$ *Cramerview Shopping Centre, 277 Main Road, Bryanston, Johannesburg; tel: 011-706 2837.* Despite the shopping-mall setting, this large, airy space is an oasis for fine Provençal cooking.

Kapitan's Café $ *11a Kort Street, central Johannesburg; tel: 011-834 8048.* Specialising in delicious curries, this establishment was a favourite haunt of attorneys Nelson Mandela and Oliver Tambo in the 1950s. Open lunchtimes only.

Linger Longer $$$ *58 Wierda Road, Wierda Valley, Sandton, Johannesburg; tel: 011-884 0465.* A long-serving and very luxurious restaurant serving exceptional French cuisine.

Osteria Tre Nonni $$ *9 Grafton Avenue, Craighall Park; tel: 011-327 0096.* Always abuzz with Italian families tucking into authentic dishes from Tuscany and Umbria.

PRETORIA

Chagall's at Toulouse $$ *Fountains Valley, Greenkloof; tel: 012-341 7511.* International and French bistro-style cooking in elegant country setting.

Gerard Moerdyk $$$ *752 Park Street, Arcadia, Pretoria; tel: 012-344 4856.* Old-fashioned, elegant restaurant that serves superbly cooked traditional South African cuisine, such as springbok pie and ostrich.

La Madeleine $$$ *122 Priory Road, Lynnwood, Pretoria; tel: 012-361 3667.* Sensational Provençal food. Simplicity is the watchword of Daniel Leusch's cooking, and it's won him many laurels. Open for dinner Tues–Sat.

The Odd Plate $$ *262 Rhino Street, Hennops Park, Ext 2, Centurion; tel: 012-654 5203.* Training restaurant for South African-born Prue Leith's College of Food and wine, set in a fine old building.

DURBAN AND ENVIRONS

Bombay Beirut $ *237 Marine Parade, Waterfront, Durban; tel: 031-332 1786.* Good Indian cuisine supplemented by an array of Lebanese dishes

Butcher Boys $$$ *170 Florida Road, Morningside; tel: 031-312 8248.* As the name suggests, an excellent venue for steaks and other meat dishes.

Cargo Hold $$ *uShaka Marine Park, Waterfront; tel: 031-328 8065.* International menu in a mock shipwreck overlooked by the shark tank of Durban's famous aquarium *(see page 50).*

Famous Fish Company $ *Point Verandah, Waterfront, Durban; tel: 031-368 1060.* Enjoy the fine seafood menu as you watch the ships go by.

Golden Chopsticks $ *Belmont Arcade, City Centre; tel: 031-332 8970.* Popular waterfront restaurant that has been serving top-notch Cantonese food for three full decades.

Harvey's $$$ *77 Goble Road, Morningside; tel: 031-312 9064.* Stylish, modern, award-winning restaurant with cutting-edge dishes. Busy and popular all the time.

Joe Kool's $ *137 Lower Marine Parade, North Beach, Durban 4001; tel: 031-332 9697.* Popular beachfront bar, restaurant and surfer hangout. Steaks, burgers, pizza and pasta.

Joop's Place $$ *Avondale Centre, Ninth Avenue, Greyville; tel: 031-312 9135.* This long-serving carnivore's favourite was rated Durban's Steakhouse of the Year in 2004. Closed Sundays.

Kaya Café $ *Bat Centre, City Centre; tel: 083-516 4582.* Inexpensive and varied menu of Zulu and other African dishes, overlooking harbour.

Lourenço Marques Café $ *Fields Hill Shopping Centre, Kloof; tel: 031-764 7899.* Bright and casual restaurant serving many dishes influenced by Portuguese colonial rule.

Marco's $$ *45 Windermere Road, Morningside; tel: 031-303 3078.* Tasty home-made pasta and a good selection of wines.

New Fish Café $$ *31 Yacht Mole, Victoria Embankment, Durban 4001; tel: 031-305 5062/3.* Top fresh seafood restaurant with spacious setting next to the yacht harbour. Open seven days a week.

Ulundi $$$ *The Royal Hotel, 267 Smith Street, Durban; tel: 031-333 6000.* Renowned curry restaurant in smart, colonial-style surroundings at The Royal Hotel *(see page 131).*

Zenbisushi $ *Wilson's Wharf, Victoria Embankment, Durban; tel: 031-307 7883.* Tasty sushi and succulent oysters overlooking the bay from the city centre. Range of sushi changes daily. Closed Monday.

PORT ELIZABETH

Bella Napoli $ *Hartman Street, Port Elizabeth; tel: 041-585 3819.* Informal Italian and Mediterranean cooking at a good price. Sunday lunch buffet.

Margot's $$ *1 Beach Road, Humewood; tel: 041-585 1000.* Creative French, Cajun and international cuisine.

The Ranch House of Steaks $$ *Corner of Russell and Rose streets, central Port Elizabeth; tel: 041-585 9684.* Mainly for steaks, any size, but some Greek and Turkish alternatives are also on the menu.

CAPE TOWN AND ENVIRONS

Africa Café $$ *110 Shortmarket Street, Heritage Square; tel: 021-422 0221.* Indigenous dishes from across the continent, served in lively, vibrant surroundings.

Biesmiellah $ *Upper Wale Street, Bo-Kaap, Cape Town; tel: 021-23 0850.* Traditional Cape Malay dishes, in the old Malay quarter (Hallal Muslim). Closed Sunday.

Blues $$$ *The Promenade, Victoria Road, Camps Bay; tel: 021-438 2040.* Californian-style cuisine in a spacious, airy room overlooking one of the world's most pristinely beautiful beaches. Always packed, so book ahead.

Boschendal Restaurant $$$ *Groot Drakenstein; tel: 021-870 4274.* Situated on the wine estate of the same name between Stellenbosch and Franschhoek, this offers first-class South African cuisine in elegant surroundings.

Buitenverwachting $$$ *Klein Constantia Road, Constantia; tel: 021-794 3522.* The name means 'beyond expectation' and that's a fair description of this wonderful restaurant set on a stunning wine estate. Impressive wine list. Closed Monday and during August.

Cape Malay Restaurant $$ *The Cellars-Hohenort Hotel, 93 Brommersvlei Road, Constantia; tel: 021-794 2137.* Traditional Cape Malay restaurant in this luxury hotel *(see page 134).* Best of the country's indigenous cuisine.

Constantia Nek $$ *Hout Bay Road, Constantia Nek; tel: 021-794 5132.* Between Hout Bay and Constantia. Specialises in functions and dinner-dances. Closed Monday.

Constantia Uitsig $$$ *Spaanschemat River Road, Constantia; tel: 021-794 4480.* This wine farm restaurant offers fine Provençal cooking where fish and game are specialities.

Floris Smit Huijs $$$ *55 Church Street, City Centre; tel: 021-423 3414.* Set in a restored 18th-century Dutch townhouse. The menus here have an African emphasis with a light modern twist. Closed Sunday.

Green Dolphin $$ *Victoria & Alfred Arcade, Cape Town; tel: 021-21 7471.* Seafood, pasta and pizza. Sometimes live jazz. Situated in the redeveloped dockside area.

Gugu Le Africa $ *Corner Spine and Iwandle roads, Khayelitsha; tel: 082-423 8479.* In the townships, a traditional Xhosa and Cape-style buffet.

JB Rivers Café and Cocktail Saloon $$ *Cavendish Square, Cape Town; tel: 021-683 0840.* New Orleans-style spicy Cajun cooking and a multitude of intriguing cocktails.

Knysna Oyster Company $ *Long St, Thesen's island, Knysna; tel: 044-382 6942.* Cheap-and-cheerful joint serving oysters cultivated in Knysna lagoon and the local draught beer.

Morton's on the Wharf $ *Shop 221, Victoria Wharf, Victoria & Alfred Waterfront; tel: 021-418 3633.* One of the best bars and restaurants crowding this thriving dock-side complex. Cajun and Creole cooking.

Panama Jack's $$ *Royal Yacht Club Basin, off Goliath Road, Dockside; tel: 021-447 3992.* Fabulous fresh seafood dishes in friendly, informal surroundings.

Le Quartier Français $$$ *16 Huguenot Street, Franschhoek; tel: 021-876 2151.* Cuisine reflecting influences of the region's original French settler families.

The Savoy Cabbage $$ *Heritage Square, 101 Hout Street, Cape Town 8001; tel: 021-424 2626.* Hearty food, sometimes in odd combinations, with notable local influence. The city-centre building is an interesting blend of old and new. Closed Sunday.

INDEX